Testimonials

"Pam Pabla's 25-year journey is more than a story about building a career in the insurance industry—it's a powerful testimony of perseverance, purpose, and faith. With honesty and grace, Pam takes us through the highs and lows of being a working mom, a woman in business, and a believer navigating real life. Her wisdom is hard-won and deeply inspiring. Whether you're in the insurance field or simply seeking encouragement in your own journey, this book will uplift, motivate, and remind you that with faith, family, and fierce determination, anything is possible!"

—Nav Sandher
Insurance Professional

"Pam Pabla's decades of experience in business and leadership are powerfully reflected in her new book, *Unshakable Leadership*. As a fellow professional in a fast-paced industry, I deeply admire her ability to lead with clarity, conviction, and care. This book is not only a reflection of her incredible journey; it's a purposeful guide rooted in real-life wisdom, built on accountability, responsibility, and faithfulness. Pam's leadership is lived, not just written about, and this book is a daily source of encouragement for anyone striving to lead with strength, humility, and purpose."

—Hardeep Ghuman
Real Estate Professional

"Knowing Pam personally and having worked closely with her and her daughter, I've witnessed the reality behind her leadership journey. Her path has involved real struggle, deep responsibility, and profound growth. The summary reflects what I already know to be true about Pam. *Unshakable Leadership* is rooted in the life of someone who has led through challenge with faith and the attitude of never giving up. Her story is one of quiet power, and I'm proud to see it shared."

—Swarna Shivdasani
Certified Yoga Therapist

"*Unshakable Leadership* is a glimpse into the life of a strong, compassionate and driven woman—Pam Pabla. Many who read this book will see a reflection of themselves and begin to appreciate the hard work, passion, and the transformational power of leadership development and growth stages in life. Her story resonates in so many spheres, providing insight and new perspectives, and challenges the reader on new ways of approach."

—Rafiqua Masih
Associate Pastor and Health & Life Coach

"*Unshakeable Leadership* is about empowering people to accomplish their goals in the midst of daunting challenges.

Pam has demonstrated this in her personal life and positive relationship with others.

Accountability, responsibility, and strong faith in God are the pillars of the leadership transformation."

—Dr. Olufemi Adegun
President, Canadian Institute of Technology,
Entrepreneurship and Management (CITEM)

"Watching Pam grow as a leader, business owner, and mom has been truly inspiring. She leads with heart, tenacity, and authenticity—qualities I know will shine through in *Unshakable Leadership*. This book is a reflection of who she is and what she stands for, and I know it will empower others to lead in their own unique way."

—Tabitha Ranga

"Pam Pabla is a bright light in every room she walks into—radiating positivity and wisdom, and inspiring vision. After collaborating with her recently, I'm excited for the many impactful projects ahead and thrilled to celebrate the launch of *Unshakeable Leadership*."

—Rina Gill

"Pam Pabla is a powerful example of what it means to lead with purpose and heart. Watching her journey as a visionary entrepreneur, devoted mother, and faith-filled leader has been deeply moving. Her chapter in *Unshakable Leadership* is honest, courageous, and packed with insight. This book will challenge and inspire you to rise with boldness and authenticity."

—Anita Punni

UNSHAKABLE LEADERSHIP

Incorporating Accountability, Responsibility, and Faithfulness to Transform Lives

PAM PABLA

10-10-10
Publishing

Unshakable Leadership: Incorporating Accountability, Responsibility, and Faithfulness to Transform Lives

www.unshakableleadershipbook.com

Copyright © 2025 Pam Pabla

Paperback ISBN: 978-1-77277-664-5

Publisher
10-10-10 Publishing
Markham, ON
Canada

Printed in Canada and the United States of America

Dedication

I dedicate this book, *Unshakable Leadership*, to my Heavenly Father—the One who called, equipped, and sustained me through every chapter of this journey. All glory belongs to You.

To my spiritual father, Pastor Prem, thank you for recognizing God's calling on my life and for speaking it into existence. Your prophetic words became the spark that led to this book. Your wisdom, faith, and covering have been a guiding light throughout this journey.

To my family—Rhea, Rupam, Taygveer, Sahib, Parm, Surinder, and our beloved Charlie—your love, prayers, patience, and presence have been my anchor and my greatest blessing.

Rhea, you are a miracle and a radiant light in our lives. Your persistence and determination inspire me every day. When you decide you want to learn something, you do it completely. Watching you capitalize on your strengths in music and math has brought us so much joy.

Rupam, your strength, compassion, and brilliance inspire me every day. You are my first world and my best friend. As I see you grow into the roles of wife and mother, I am incredibly proud of you. Together, we have been through plenty of firsts, and I am blessed to continue this journey with you.

Taygveer, your heart, character, and quiet strength have been among the greatest gifts to our family. You stepped into our lives not as a son-in-law but as a true son. Your love, respect, and integrity have touched me deeply.

Sahib, you are the blessing in our family's lives and the most beautiful gift from God.

Parm, your unwavering belief in me, your love, and your steady strength have lifted me more times than you know. Thank you for walking this journey by my side with grace and faith.

Mom (Surinder), your wisdom, resilience, and unconditional love are the roots that ground me. Your prayers have carried me, and your example has shaped me to be the woman I am today.

To my beloved father, Harmohinder, though you are no longer with us, your strength, values, and love continue to live on in me. I carry your legacy in my heart every day.

Charlie, your gentle presence reminds me daily of the beauty in stillness, loyalty, and joy.

To every leader who desires to rise with accountability, responsibility, and faithfulness, this book was written with you in mind.

May it ignite your purpose, challenge your perspective, and inspire you to lead with heart.

"Leadership is not about success;
it is the legacy you leave by the life you live."

—Pam Pabla

Table of Contents

Part Four

Part Five

Foreword

Leadership is about more than giving direction or assigning tasks; it means leading according to your core values, in order to inspire and motivate those around you. For Pam Pabla, quality leadership involves accountability, responsibility, and faithfulness. As she shares parts of her family's story, Pam illustrates these aspects of leadership in *Unshakable Leadership: Incorporating Accountability, Responsibility, and Faithfulness to Transform Lives.* With practical and actionable steps, Pam will demonstrate:

- How accountability starts with you as the leader

- How early intervention is essential to success, regardless of the circumstances

- The importance of responsibility at every level of leadership

- How faithfulness ties different aspects of leadership together, including your honesty and integrity

- How to take your vision and lead with purpose

- How a growth mindset is key to tapping into the creativity and learning opportunities surrounding you and those you are leading

In *Unshakable Leadership: Incorporating Accountability, Responsibility, and Faithfulness to Transform Lives*, Pam highlights the importance of being open-minded, positive, and willing to tap into others' experience and knowledge. Using her own experience as a parent and business owner, Pam highlights how you can lead with accountability, responsibility, and faithfulness, transforming lives no matter the circumstances.

—Loral Langemeier
The Millionaire Maker

Introduction

Leadership is more than just a title or position in a career. At its core, leadership encompasses a way of living, a mindset that influences how you treat others and how you can influence them with your own journey of growth. My name is **Pam Pabla**. I have spent the last 25 years navigating leadership and faithfulness, acting with integrity and mindfulness while holding myself and others accountable. As a business owner, I have built a career on the principles of Accountability, Responsibility, and Faithfulness, allowing those principles to guide me in every aspect of my life.

Leaders face multiple challenges as they guide others, knowing their decisions can have a profound impact on them. Their actions inspire integrity and loyalty from others or degrade it. True leadership is not about having power over others but empowering them through acts of service and staying true to your course with faithfulness, even when the path is challenging. That doesn't mean you never adapt or make changes once you make a decision. However, once a decision is made, others should be able to count on you to keep your word and follow through.

For many leaders, changing circumstances require shifts in their thinking. However, if they are unwilling to be humble and acknowledge their own need to learn and grow, these leaders will be unable to adapt, and that will eventually impact every aspect of their business.

While my focus incorporates principles learned through my years as a business leader, these principles can be applied in any part of your life where you are called to lead and influence others. The goal is to find ways to utilize accountability, responsibility, and faithfulness to serve with integrity, regardless of whether it is in your family, business, or community.

As a parent, your example is influencing your children, helping them to learn how to lead effectively and with purpose and integrity. Leadership at every level involves being willing to step up, while also staying faithful to your values with each decision. Your actions today will help you shape your future, and the habits you build now will determine the kind of leader you become and how you influence the leaders of the future.

Together, we will explore the mindset required for **unshakable** leadership, the power of positivity to stay resilient, and the infinite power of thoughts to influence outcomes and shape your path to success, no matter the circumstances or challenges you face.

Through reflective exercises meant to assist you in exploring your leadership style and mindset, you will uncover the framework to:

- Stay grounded in your principles when the stakes are high.
- Adapt to change without losing sight of your vision.

- Inspire and empower those around you with empathy and purpose.

Leadership is not about reaching the top but about the process of who you become along the way. If you seek to build a foundation that is **unshakable**, purposeful, and aligned with higher values, this book is meant for you.

My hope is that it will inspire you to embrace leadership as an opportunity, one with the power to transform lives, businesses, and legacies. Let's embark on this journey together to build the **unshakable** foundation to lead with Accountability, Responsibility, and Faithfulness!

—Pam Pabla
Author | Business Leader | Faithful Parent

The Core Pillars of Leadership

- **Accountability** – Taking ownership of your decisions even amid uncertainty and pressure.

- **Responsibility** – Leading with integrity to ensure that your actions fulfill your tasks, and your choices are in the best interest of yourself and others.

- **Faithfulness** – Trusting in a vision beyond the physical realm allows hope and perseverance to guide you through life.

Part One

Chapter 1

Reality of Life–A Parent's Vision & Leadership

"As leaders and parents, we hold the power to make our vision a reality; it all starts with us."
—Pam Pabla

1

Embracing Uncertainty

I want you to think back to the early days of your family. You likely had a vision for how you wanted to parent your children, the values you wanted to embrace, and the type of influence you wanted to have. Along the way, you dream about what you want your children to achieve, envisioning their first steps, milestones, and successes, filled with joy, hope, and the endless possibilities of this new life. It is a beautiful vision, but life has a way of unfolding that can shift even the best-laid plans and visions, forcing you to adjust, adapt, and even improvise.

I was just such a parent, excited for the future of this child. When my child reached 18 months, I received the diagnosis that shifted my world off its axis. My amazing child was diagnosed with autism spectrum disorder (ASD). In that moment, everything I had dreamed was shattered and replaced by uncertainty, along with fear of the unknown. I was also dealing with grief, something not often discussed, as I grappled with my child's new future, the loss of what could have been, and the challenges that lay ahead.

This could have been the moment despair set in, drowning my ability to move forward and lead effectively. Instead of dwelling on shattered dreams, I chose to reinvent myself, which came with a lot of self-discovery and new dreams for my child and me.

Truthfully, when you sit in the doctor's office, hearing the diagnosis, it feels as if the focus is only on what your child cannot do or the challenges they will face. It is steeped in negativity and limitations. My child was now just a diagnosis, a bundle of symptoms that was no longer seen as an individual. As a parent, I saw not my child's limitations but something else. It was a mindset shift, but I refused to focus only on the challenges of the diagnosis, but rather on their unique strengths and hidden potential. This was not about survival but about finding a way to thrive through leadership, resilience, and unconditional love.

Through my unwavering determination, I began to see myself as more than a parent; I became an active guide in shaping my child's future. I became my child's greatest advocate by paving the way for their growth in directions others or myself could have never imagined.

With every challenge, I learned to advocate effectively, navigate complex systems, and approach each situation with patience and resilience. I found strength in the smallest victories, in the moments where my child's laughter replaced my fears, and in achieving milestones that defied every expectation. Advocacy was not only about securing external support. It was about empowering my child to see their own limitless potential. This journey has redefined love, resilience, and faith for me in ways that have transformed my child and myself. My purpose is redefined, a sharp and clear vision of what I am meant to do with my life. Every aspect of this unique journey proved that unwavering love, perseverance, and faith can transform challenges into extraordinary possibilities.

You might be wondering what this has to do with leadership. At a fundamental level, I was the leader, the one my child was following. My mindset, words, and actions were the example my child was going to follow. If I fell into despair and gave up, so would my child. I am the leader, shaping my child's values and view of themselves.

Staying positive and maintaining a mindset steeped in values and purpose can be challenging, especially when you feel overwhelmed by the daily tasks in front of you. Let's talk about what a day in the life can be like for parents, especially those whose children are facing unique circumstances or medical conditions that make everyday tasks more challenging.

A Day in the Life

One of the first challenges is making time for myself, to recharge and prepare for the day. When I don't make time for myself, it is hard to bring my best to my child and advocate effectively.

Everyone's routine is different, but I encourage you to carve out time for yourself, preferably before the chaos begins. You might use this time to reflect on your blessings, meditate, and relax your mind. I use this time to connect with the Creator, showing my gratitude for being able to see another day filled with opportunities. While it might be easy to tell yourself that there is no time in the day for you, the truth is that without this time, you will not give your family or others your best.

There is an expression, "Fill the cup you pour from." As a leader, it is critical you do that every day. Think of your car. If you don't make sure it has gas, then eventually, you will end up stranded on the side of the road. As your child's advocate and a leader in your home, fill your car with gas for the journey by taking time for yourself daily.

My day involves navigating my child's therapy and the obligations associated with it. After all, the time with the therapist is relatively short, so my consistency in practicing what we learned is key to building and maintaining my child's momentum and progress. On top of that, I still have the necessary tasks to keep our home and my business functioning. Multi-tasking is a fact of life. We might be waiting for an appointment, and I am ordering groceries to pick up later or checking in with my business. Part of my career focus involves growing my network with other professionals to expand my business.

Evenings are spent interacting with other individuals, exchanging positive advice, sharing successes, and gaining strength from my community, one that understands the joys and perils of this journey. Truthfully, these interactions are essential to my self-care, as I gain encouragement to keep going, both personally and professionally.

After everyone is settled for the night, I wind down, reflecting on the small victories throughout the day. Instead of letting my mind dwell on what went wrong or the struggles, I focus on the blessings and what went right. That is not to say as a leader, I put my head in the sand and ignore the challenges we might have faced. I don't. Instead, I focus on finding ways to break through the challenge, gathering information and marshaling resources, so we can move forward. Dwelling on failures or mistakes often puts your mindset into a negative spiral, which is not helpful to nurturing growth in yourself and those around you.

Progress is always possible, and my relentless efforts are feeding that progress daily. To truly embrace leadership, you need to expect failure and be open to learning from it. At the same time, you cannot dwell on failures or mistakes, allowing them to define you as a leader. People are inspired by leaders who demonstrate grace and determination, picking themselves up when they fall, with accountability and respect for others.

Highlight: Days can be exhausting, but achieving small wins will make them meaningful. Your vision should shift to protecting yourself and your loved ones so that you can **thrive, discover, and lead with confidence.**

Early Intervention: The Foundation for Success

One thing that became clear to me early on is that **timing is everything.** The earlier I could address my child's needs, the better the chances for meaningful development. Early intervention became my guiding principle to achieve my goals. Having early intervention implemented for my child meant that I could pursue my business milestones at the right time of my life, while helping my child to thrive in their own life.

I sought out therapies, specialists, and tailored programs that focused on my child's development. Whether speech therapy to unlock communication, occupational therapy to develop motor skills, or social programs to foster connection, every action was deliberate and hopeful. The goal was to start intervention in areas where my child might struggle more, thus giving the extra support needed before and during specific developmental periods.

Early intervention wasn't just about skill-building for my child; it was about **unlocking my potential as a business owner and a mother.** It was about showing my child and myself that we are capable of greatness, even if our path looked different from the one I had envisioned. We saw early intervention as a way to problem solve, to move past the negative future outlook to find rays of hope and build my child's confidence.

> **Highlight:** Life does not always go as planned, but what is planned is how we adapt to our stories and use our experiences to make great successes out of them.

When you are in a leadership role, whether in your family or a professional setting, you model the mindset for those you are leading. Others will follow your lead, either into a growth mindset or a limited and failure-based one. What does this mean for you as a leader? It translates into a conscious choice you make regarding your mindset and how you showcase that mindset, because it will define the tone and style of your leadership.

Early intervention helped me demonstrate a proactive approach while also showing how you can actively search for support instead of waiting for others to see your struggles and provide assistance. I saw early intervention as a way to forecast, look for potential issues, and find solutions before they impeded my progress.

Leaders serve their families and others by being accountable for their choices and all aspects of their journey. That said, you don't have to wait for problems to arise before addressing them. Seek out those with experience in these areas and tap into their experience as part of your growth journey.

Use interventions to help others learn the skills they need, while also highlighting what they are doing well. This type of targeted early intervention will build their confidence in their abilities. Confident people are willing to take responsibility for their actions and take the risks necessary to achieve long-term success.

Take a moment to think of areas where your business might have struggled in the past. Could you promote early intervention training to eliminate some of those struggles, thus making processes easier to follow, resulting in greater accuracy? Could early intervention be incorporated into your onboarding of new team members? Is there a regular training program in place to keep upgrading your employees' skills? If so, is it effective? Do you participate in training programs with those you lead, thus helping them to see you as an accountable and responsible leader?

These questions are meant to assist you in finding ways to incorporate early intervention strategies, therefore helping you to discover more of your team's talents and giving you opportunities to serve them with growth-oriented leadership strategies.

Discovering Leadership in the Child

As a mother leaning into my role as a guide and advocate, I noticed something incredible: **My child possessed leadership qualities.**

While I was the adult, meant to provide security and consistency during the most challenging times, I also was put in a position to learn from my child. Many of the qualities demonstrated by my child became a part of my leadership foundation. Here are a few of the qualities my child demonstrated daily that helped me to grow as a parent and leader:

- **Persistence**: Tasks that once seemed challenging, such as tying shoes or completing a puzzle, became milestones achieved through determination and repetition. This persistence was a quiet form of leadership.

- **Empathy**: In moments of connection, my child demonstrated a deep sensitivity towards others. Whether offering a comforting gesture to a sibling or responding to someone's emotions, this empathy was a reminder that leadership is often rooted in understanding and care for those around us. That is a principle of my own business and one that continues to benefit us as we work toward shared goals. After all, they have lives outside of my business, so showing empathy as a leader helps them to feel heard and contributes to greater loyalty in the long run.

- **Creativity**: From expressing themselves through art and music to finding unique solutions to challenges, my child's creativity became a strength that redefined what it meant to be able to discover leadership skills within themselves. Celebrating creativity and not being quick to dismiss the power of thinking outside of conventional methods assists me in leading others effectively as we adapt to shifting industries and demand. Be open to the creativity available to you and do not be quick to assume you are the only one with viable ideas and solutions.

By focusing on these strengths, I began to foster leadership within my child and myself. I taught my children to recognize their value, embrace their individuality, and trust in their abilities, just as they taught me. It was about helping each other lead our lives with confidence and purpose within ourselves and society regardless of the circumstances. The confidence that developed as we pushed through the challenges with persistence, empathy, and creativity fosters resilience when life takes new twists and turns. Are you equipping others for future challenges by building their confidence right now?

> **Highlight:** Confidence does not solely come from within; it comes from the experiences and challenges we go through in life that push us to be the best version of ourselves.

Building confidence comes in a variety of ways, but as a leader, you need to be persistent, empathic, and creative to build confidence in yourself and others. To truly be a leader with accountability, responsibility, and faithfulness, you need to be looking for ways to serve, applauding the efforts of others and finding ways to increase their skills and confidence.

Leadership Parallel: Lessons for Us All

My journey mirrors what all great leaders experience: Plans get disrupted, obstacles arise, but true leadership lies in how we respond in these moments of uncertainty to move forward successfully, helping others thrive and achieve their goals.

At this point, take a moment to reflect on your leadership style. Understanding your personal strengths and weaknesses from a leadership point of view can assist you to determine where your focus should lie. The areas discussed below are signs of an effective leader. How would you rate yourself?

1. **Adapt to changing circumstances.** When the original vision no longer fits, they redefine it. How do you react to changes? Are you comfortable doing things the way they have always been done, or are you open to new ideas and fresh perspectives?

2. **Uncover strengths, not limitations.** They focus on what is possible and build on it. When someone demonstrates a greater level of ability in one area, do you encourage them to develop it further, or do you feel threatened by their success and strengths?

3. **Empower others to lead.** Whether it's a team member, a child, or a community, leaders bring out the best in those around them. Are you focused on growing leaders, allowing others to expand their leadership abilities, or do you find yourself holding on to key aspects of your process, blocking others from developing further?

If you see yourself struggling in one of these areas, do not be discouraged. After all, my child exposed many aspects of my leadership style that could improve. Knowledge is power, especially if you embrace the opportunity to grow and change direction. Leaders are not static, but they fluidly shift with the times to bring their best selves to their families and their businesses.

While I want you to reflect in this section, understand that the next section provides action items, helping you to develop more fully in the areas of accountability, responsibility, and faithfulness. When you are open to learning and growing, then it becomes easier to incorporate these qualities and lead with integrity and purpose.

Key Lessons for Leaders

1. **Vision Is Vital—But Stay Flexible**
   Dreams are ever changing; great leaders understand that flexibility is a strength, not a weakness.

2. **Early Intervention Sparks Momentum**
   Taking an action early can lay the groundwork for everlasting success.

3. **Focus on Strengths, Not Limitations**
   My beliefs in my child's strengths mirrors what great leaders do: They see potential where others may see problems or burdens.

Interactive Reflection for Readers

Journal Prompt:

Reflect on a time when you had to adapt your vision to unexpected circumstances. How did you uncover strengths in yourself or others?

Write about an area in your life where early action could create meaningful change. What steps can you take today?

Action Step:

Identify one person in your life with untapped potential. Have a conversation with them about their strengths and encourage them to pursue growth.

Progress Requires Patience and Hope

My journey illustrates that life's challenges are not obstacles; they are opportunities to discover new strengths, redefine success, and inspire leadership in extraordinary ways. My commitment to early intervention and focus on my child's potential exemplify resilience amidst uncertainty and the essence of genuine leadership.

True leadership calls for **patience, resilience, and inner peace**—a peace born from recognizing that every step forward, no matter the speed, is a step toward progress. It recognizes the power of growth, while understanding that the best leaders look for opportunities to serve and empower others.

As you continue reading, remember that **Accountability, Responsibility, and Faithfulness**, paired with **Mindset, Positivity,**

and the Power of Thoughts, form a foundation of unshakable leadership. Using these tools, you can embrace life's uncertainties, foster growth in yourself and others, and lead with purpose and confidence for years to come!

Notes

_____

_____

_____

_____

_____

_____

_____

_____

_____

_____

_____

_____

_____

_____

Part Two

Chapter 2

Accountability–Taking Ownership of Your Vision

*"Accountability is fulfilling obligations by taking ownership
and responsibility of your own actions and results."*
– Pam Pabla

2

At a fundamental level, every leader who is successful, both personally and professionally, embraces accountability for themselves and expects it from others. Accountability is defined as being responsible for what you do and able to give a satisfactory reason for it, according to Merriam Webster. As a leader, you have the ability to hold others accountable for a defined set of duties and require an accounting regarding whether those duties have been fulfilled or not.

Within your family, parenting requires you to set expectations for your children, then hold them accountable for meeting those expectations and, as the person in a position of authority, you have the right to discipline or reward based on how well those expectations are met.

As a parent and business owner, I have to hold people accountable; otherwise, my family and business suffer. However, those within my business and family do not always appreciate being held accountable. Excuses abound for why things are not done, and blame quickly gets spread around to those.

When there are a number of excuses, I have to work with them and cut through the excuses to find the reasons why tasks were not accomplished and provide consequences where necessary. Defining true barriers to completing tasks or meeting expectations, then coming up with and implementing solutions, is essential to implementing accountability with yourself and those around you.

Embracing Accountability

Accountability is the cornerstone of leadership. It is the ability to take full ownership of one's actions, decisions, and outcomes. Accountability is not just about fulfilling responsibilities but about maintaining an unshakable commitment to one's vision without any hindering challenges.

While, as a leader, you are accountable to yourself for completing specific tasks, those are part of a larger purpose or greater goal. For instance, when I set out to improve sales at my business, I set goals regarding how many sales calls I want to complete each day, how many contacts with customers I want to complete each week, and set numbers for my sales personnel as well. Holding us accountable to reaching those numbers translates into reaching the larger goal, which is increased sales.

Being accountable means recognizing all the steps necessary to achieve your vision, then setting up a strategy that allows you to complete those steps in a reasonable timeframe. As a leader, being accountable means looking at the bigger picture and holding yourself to a course of action that allows you to turn that big picture into reality for your company or family.

From a spiritual perspective, accountability reflects a profound respect for the universe's calling that guides your journey. It requires aligning with your daily choices, which determine the bigger picture.

Accountability bridges intention and impact, enabling you to take charge of your life and inspire others to do the same.

Accountability Through a Parent's Eyes

As a parent navigating the challenges of raising a child with autism, accountability takes on a profound meaning. It becomes more than simply meeting responsibilities; it transforms into a relentless pursuit of your child's potential. I do not resign myself to societal expectations or limitations. Instead, I take ownership of my child's future, knowing that the key to unlocking their strengths lies in my willingness to advocate, adapt, and lead with unwavering determination for years to come.

My vision for my child is not about "fixing" them but about finding and nurturing the **unique leadership qualities** they already possess. I see beyond the diagnosis, the barriers, and the possibilities. Early **intervention** is the foundation upon which this vision is built.

This type of accountability also shapes how my child sees herself. I am modeling for her a way of being in the world, of acknowledging the challenges but not allowing them to become barriers that keep her from achieving her goals and dreams. Your mindset plays an essential role in this process. Without the right mindset, you will lead your child into thinking that they are limited by their diagnosis, instead of being empowered by it. How does accountability help me with this process?

Uncovering Strengths and Leadership Within the Child

Accountability drives me to focus not on what my child cannot do, but on what they are able to do. I dedicate myself to discovering and developing my child's strengths, knowing that these talents hold the key to their confidence and future success. Here are just a few of those strengths and their critical role in building accountability. Remember, focusing on strengths does not mean we ignore weaknesses; we find ways to utilize their strengths more fully, while also working to improve in the weak areas.

- **Persistence**: I celebrate my child's determination to master tasks that once seemed impossible. Whether it's completing a new skill or extracurricular activities, their persistence demonstrates resilience, a core trait of leadership that also taught me not to limit myself. Instead, I focused on persisting to achieve my professional goals. When I was not immediately successful or obstacles appeared, that persistence helped me to stay resilient.

- **Empathy**: In moments of connection, my child shows a unique ability to sense the emotions of others. This quiet empathy becomes a powerful leadership quality, fostering understanding and compassion. As a professional, working to understand the people in my business, having grace, and recognizing circumstances can impact their ability to focus. While holding them accountable for their tasks, empathy helps me to be flexible where I can, working to be empathic to the needs and feelings of those I lead.

- **Creativity**: From problem solving to self-expression, my child's creativity shines as a reminder that leadership is not confined to traditional paths. It's about finding innovative ways to overcome challenges. This also holds true from a business standpoint as it helped me to take challenges and use them as opportunities to elevate myself and my business. I embrace the creativity of others, not being quick to assume my way is the only way to achieve our professional goals. By being open to hearing others' ideas, I give my business a chance to grow. Accountability often starts by recognizing that I don't have all the answers and embracing the creativity of others' perspectives and experiences.

Leadership does not look the same for everyone, as it is unique based on individual experiences. For my child, it may mean embracing their individuality, building confidence in their abilities, and leading their life with purpose and authenticity. My accountability keeps me moving forward, even when progress feels slow, because it focuses me on the progress I have made in reaching my goals, which motivates me to keep moving forward.

> **Highlight:** Finding a cause and cure for autism is a long journey. To achieve it, it takes a dedicated community of accountable families, professionals, and caregivers sharing this common goal.

We consider ourselves to be among the leaders of this community, open to new ideas and exploring the strengths of our children, instead of focusing on the perceived weaknesses. Helping them to achieve their goals builds confidence. At the same time, their persistence keeps them progressing. Finally, when we show empathy for their feelings and experiences, we model how they can do this for others, thus leading with purpose and kindness.

The Power of Early Intervention

As a parent and business owner, I recognize that ignoring small problems or issues can lead to much bigger and more expensive problems down the road. Look around your business. Each aspect of it is an investment of time, energy, and financial resources. Your strategic plan helps you to determine where investment needs to happen and prioritize your resources accordingly.

However, when a small problem arises, you might need to shift your priorities to address it right away. Problems or issues that are continually ignored often grow, requiring more resources to address them later on than addressing them early.

For my child, I wanted to help her reach her full potential and succeed. That meant giving her the skills and tools to navigate a world not built to accommodate her unique challenges. I also recognized that she would be better able to grasp these new skills if we started teaching them to her right away.

The development of a child happens over time, but certain skills need to be learned in order for them to advance to the next stage of their development. For instance, when your child is learning to walk, they first had to learn balance by strengthening their back muscles to sit up without your assistance. Then they began to learn how to coordinate the movements of their arms and legs, giving them the ability to crawl. Building up the strength of their legs allowed them to pull themselves up and eventually stand. Finally, all these skills were combined and they took their first steps.

No child can skip the steps within this learning process. While they might learn differently, evidence of all these steps can be found in their ability to walk. As a parent, you work with them on all these steps, helping them to master these new skills and abilities. If you notice they are having difficulty, your invention helps them to figure it out and get back on track.

Early intervention was key for my child to meet critical milestones. Had we not moved forward with early interventions and therapies, her progress could have been limited. One of the things I realized early on was that music was my child's language. When my child was small, we were at someone's home when my child sat down at their piano and started playing. My child was able to hear something played one time and play it back. This strength was my child's connection to music and the ability to play it with feeling and creativity. Our early interventions went beyond working with my child on specific skills for development, but also included tapping into her strengths to aid her development, like music and math.

The challenge was there, but I saw the importance of continuing to help my child interact with the world. Rather than bemoaning the challenge, I saw it as an opportunity. For instance, my child had a lot of energy, so they went to swimming classes, which allowed them to burn that energy off. Math was a strength, so I enrolled my child in an abacus program where numbers and math were constantly done. Instead of trying to make my child fit into a certain mold, as a leader, I shifted my focus to their strengths.

As a business leader, I also saw the importance of early interventions for my employees and how they helped them achieve success. When you see a problem brewing, be accountable to yourself to address it right away. Sit down with your key individuals in your business and figure out the problem's negative impacts, as well as brainstorm potential solutions.

You might be surprised at the solutions they offer. Some might not be costly to implement, but they will ultimately save your business money and increase productivity over time.

Early intervention is my primary tool for success with my child and business. I recognized that addressing my child's needs early on unlocked their potential and paved the way for their long-term growth. Accountability inspires me to seek out therapies, specialists, and resources that will support my child's development at early stages.

- **Speech and Language Development**: I prioritize interventions that help my child communicate, knowing that self-expression is vital to building confidence and forming relationships.

- **Emotional Regulation**: I work with therapists to teach my child tools for managing emotions, laying the foundation for resilience and self-leadership.

- **Social Skills**: Through playgroups and social programs, I helped my child navigate interactions, fostering connections and encouraging a sense of belonging.

I also realized that early intervention could lead to more tremendous success. One of the most significant ways is through training that fits a pre-defined professional growth trajectory. When I encourage my employees to increase their knowledge and grow their skill sets, I am giving my business a greater number of resources to tap into, creating a growth situation that leads to success.

Dedication to early intervention is not just about milestones; it's about **empowerment**. By taking early steps and showing consistency, I give my child the tools she needs to thrive, paving the way for a brighter future where she can lead a life on her own terms.

On a professional level, early intervention through targeted training allows me to address obstacles with meaningful solutions that support long-lasting growth. Giving others opportunities to learn new skills, or helping them develop the skills they already have, empowers them to find solutions, be creative, and be confident in their abilities. When you are confident and capable, you value accountability because it assists you in staying on track with your goals. For my family and my business, being empowered happens on multiple levels. I encourage you to empower those around you because, when you do that as a leader, you inspire others to give their best and hold themselves accountable for achieving their goals and staying on task.

Early intervention is one piece of the puzzle to creating meaningful accountability, but it is also important that you identify potential excuses and triggers that can impede your progress. When a trigger is identified, you can develop strategies to address it and maintain your progress versus being sidetracked when you face a setback. The reality is that life happens, and it brings out the unexpected. When you have strategies and coping skills, you navigate the unexpected more effectively and maintain your progress instead of losing ground.

A person commits to improving their health but faces setbacks—skipped workouts, late-night snacks, or self-doubt. Instead of giving up, they take accountability by identifying triggers, adjusting their approach, and seeking support from friends or a coach.

Being intentional about setting goals, taking action, and strategizing to address triggers or potential setbacks empowers you to lead confidently and thus generate success. It allows you to see the potential in others and nurture it, not just through your words but through your actions. Accountability empowers you as you empower others. When they see you holding yourself accountable, it becomes easier for them to embrace accountability for themselves.

> **Lesson:** Accountability bridges the gap between intention and action, enabling personal transformation over time.

Building Accountability in Leadership: Action Steps

How can you more effectively foster accountability within your leadership and model it for your family and employees. Here are a few practical action steps that allow you to consciously incorporate accountability into your leadership style, thus making it a core pillar of your leadership.

1. **Set Clear Expectations**

   - **Define Roles**: Whether at home, work, or in the community, clarity creates a shared vision.

   - **Consistency**: Schedule regular check-ins to track progress and address obstacles.

2. **Embrace Continuous Growth**

   - **Feedback Loops**: Encourage input from peers, mentors, and those you lead to enhance your approach.

   - **Lifelong Learning**: View every experience, success, or failure as an opportunity to grow.

3. **Focus on Collective Responsibility**

   - **Open Communication**: Create a safe space for discussions about challenges and breakthroughs.

   - **Empathy in Leadership**: Compassion fosters trust and encourages others to take accountability for their roles.

4. **Own Outcomes**

   - **Celebrate Successes**: Be the first to recognize and praise collective achievements.

   - **Acknowledge Challenges**: Take responsibility for setbacks and shift quickly to problem solving.

Why Accountability Matters: Takeaways

1. **Builds Trust and Credibility**

   Leaders who express accountability set a powerful example, fostering trust and inspiring others to follow suit.

2. **Elevates Team and Community Spirit**

   Accountability invites collaboration and collective ownership, reducing conflict and enhancing unity.

3. **Fosters Sustainable Success**

   When leaders consistently align actions and accountability with their vision, they create an environment of integrity and stability that supports long-term growth.

Reflection and Action

Journal Prompt:

Think of a situation where accountability has been weak in your life. What fears or habits have held you back from taking full ownership? What small steps can you take today to embrace accountability in this area?

Action Step:

Identify one goal or promise you've delayed. Write down three actions you can take to restart your journey, and share your commitment with someone who can support you.

Extended Exercise:

Daily Reflection: At the end of each day, jot down one action you're proud of and one area where you could improve.

Weekly Alignment: Evaluate whether your choices align with your vision. Adjust as needed to stay on course.

Conclusion: Reflections on Personal and Professional Accountability

Accountability is not just a task; it's a principle that shapes who we are as leaders and individuals. As a parent reflecting on this chapter, accountability means taking full ownership of a child's future and relentlessly advocating for their strengths through early intervention. As a business owner, accountability means encouraging others by empowering them to learn and then utilize those new skills to grow professionally. Doing so fosters an environment built around growth that encourages creativity in addressing problems and productivity as you reach for new goals. Remember, as a leader, you have to prioritize others to maximize their effectiveness. Accountability assists you to avoid becoming distracted by triggers and setbacks, creating an environment and mindset that fosters improvement and progress.

As you move forward, remember that accountability is the first pillar in a broader leadership framework paired with responsibility and faithfulness. When parenting, in professional settings, or in personal growth, accountability ensures you lead with purpose and authenticity.

Notes

_____

_____

_____

_____

_____

_____

_____

_____

_____

_____

_____

_____

_____

_____

Chapter 3

Responsibility

"Responsibility is fulfilling your purpose in life."
– Pam Pabla

3

Responsibility is a word we hear often when it comes to fulfilling and managing life's tasks. It also plays a role in our relationships, as we take responsibility for what we say and do, which impacts others personally and professionally.

This quality of responsibility can refer to moral, legal, or mental accountability, along with reliability and trustworthiness. When you are responsible, you are answerable or accountable for something within your power, control, or management. As a responsible individual, you can recognize and accept the consequences of your decisions and actions. It involves more than just completing tasks or fulfilling your assignments; it incorporates your level of commitment.

Serving Others with Purpose

Responsibility is more than a task or obligation; it is a commitment to actively shape your life and the lives of those around you through care and service. At its core, responsibility means using your talents, resources, and influence to nurture growth, solve challenges, and create opportunities to thrive.

From a spiritual perspective, responsibility acknowledges the sacred interconnection between people. Your choices, whether small or big, impact your family, community, and the broader world. It is not just about doing what needs to be done but about embracing a service mindset and uplifting those around you.

For those who lead with purpose, responsibility acknowledges that you cannot always do what you prefer, but that to be a good leader within your family, business, and community means taking the needs of others into account before you make your decisions. Being responsible focuses on others and how you are accountable to them.

It can be easy to say that you are responsible, yet make excuses for your behavior and pointing fingers at others. Acting entitled or taking on the role of a victim is the opposite of being responsible, because those who follow that path opt to not acknowledge how their words and actions impact those around them.

Stop for a moment and think about your family and business. In each area, you are responsible for others, but what those responsibilities entail vary. For instance, a business owner is responsible for paying his employees on time, ensuring they have the right equipment and resources, and also providing a safe working environment.

Parents, on the other hand, are responsible for caring for their children's basic needs from babyhood to young adulthood. They are responsible not only for their physical needs but their mental, emotional, and spiritual ones. For a parent, taking on the role of raising children means investing your time, energy, and resources into assisting this person to grow into a contributing member of society, while celebrating their unique attributes.

Yet, for those of us who have a child with autism or other challenges, the responsibilities of parenting become more profound and require you to tap into strengths and skills as a leader that you may have not even realized you had.

Responsibility Through a Parent's Eyes

Responsibility takes on a profound meaning for a parent raising a child with autism. For me, it is not just about providing care; it is about **building a foundation for my child's success** by uncovering their strengths and unlocking their leadership potential.

My role as a parent is to meet my child's immediate needs and allow my purpose to be limitless. I see myself as my child's greatest advocate, teacher, and guide, responsible for supporting my child and creating an environment where they feel safe, grow, thrive, and lead a fulfilling life.

What can make this aspect of parenting more challenging is that your child might not communicate or express themselves in neurotypical ways. You become responsible for fostering and building communication, so you understand what they need in their environment to be healthy and thriving.

That is not always easy to do. It means leading with patience and grace, setting an example for your other children who might struggle to be patient or have grace for their siblings. Being different can be difficult in certain situations. Not every place in society is going to make accommodations for my child, so I have to be responsible enough to give her the tools to navigate a world not built for someone who is neurodivergent.

My journey is one of patience and purpose, where every action reflects my unwavering belief in my child's potential and gives her the skills to craft a life she loves.

- **Early Intervention as the Cornerstone**: Time is vital for fluent development and growth for any child. Early intervention enables me to address challenges and foster strengths during the most critical years of development.

- **Fostering Independence**: I am determined to provide my child with the skills they need to navigate the world confidently. From communication to emotional regulation, I ensure they are prepared to face life's challenges.

- **Building Confidence**: Focusing on my child's unique abilities, such as creativity, empathy, or persistence, I nurture a sense of self-worth and leadership that empowers them to embrace their individuality, as well as teaches them to embrace the individuality of others.

> **Highlight**: Our unique challenges give us responsibility in life, which becomes our strength to be an unshakable leader.

As a business owner, you can also look to develop these skills and qualities within others. When you see problems or issues developing, take the time to address them early on. Early intervention can prevent issues from developing into larger problems that disrupt the flow and productivity within your business.

Secondly, always be open to letting other individuals take the lead as opportunities arise. Micromanagement does not foster a close and productive team; it erodes how the team works together. Your business is like a symphony, and micromanaging makes it difficult for you to function harmoniously and make beautiful music together.

Instead, when you allow them to work independently, you build their confidence, which positively impacts their productivity. When you give others the chance to work independently or take a leadership role, they develop skills to help them navigate the challenges that naturally happen throughout the course of running a business.

While I believe in building up others by focusing on their strengths, you must also be responsible for pointing out areas where they can improve. Creating plans to help others grow professionally will positively impact their confidence. Truly, responsible leadership focuses on how you can grow team members in a meaningful way and begin to see the leadership qualities you are fostering through your decisions.

Discovering Leadership in My Child

Through my dedication and perseverance, I began to see glimmers of leadership within my child, qualities that, when nurtured, can shape them into a confident and capable individual.

- **Strength in Persistence**: Tasks that once seemed impossible, such as learning to tie shoes, complete a sentence, or master a skill, became milestones of resilience.

My child's determination reflects the heart of leadership: refusing to give up, even when progress is slow.

- **Empathy as a Superpower**: My child demonstrates profound empathy, offering comfort and connection in ways that touch those around them in the most innocent form of human connections. This ability is a foundational trait of great leaders.

- **Creativity and Problem Solving**: Through art, play, and music, to name a few, my child's creativity and imagination become a source of strength that they use to express themselves. This shows that leadership is not about following a set path but about finding innovative ways to navigate challenges.

My focus is not on molding my child to fit societal expectations but on helping them discover their own voice, strengths, and leadership potential. This is responsibility in its highest form: **empowering someone to unlock their potential to lead a life with confidence and purpose.**

The Essence of Responsibility

The most responsible people are often not focused on themselves or receiving honors or accolades. Their goal is to learn and grow, leading with humility and a belief in serving the needs of others within their families, businesses, and communities. In teaching my children about responsibility, I also highlighted how important it is to keep your word and how that contributes to your reputation and is a sign of your character.

Being responsible is not truly about completing a list of tasks but incorporates accountability with empathy and humility. It is about being honest with yourself regarding your strengths and weaknesses, while also being excited and supportive when others bring different knowledge, experiences, and strengths to the table.

In some cases, responsibility is based on being realistic about what is possible and not forcing people into roles that do not suit them. As a business leader, I realized that my parenting journey helped me to grasp this concept. My child didn't fit into a typical developmental journey, so instead of trying to squeeze her into that journey, I accepted that her journey was unique and shifted my expectations accordingly.

When at work with your employees, be open to evaluating who fits best in various positions. While providing opportunities for growth can help productivity, be open to adjusting the responsibilities or roles of your employees so your business can benefit more fully from their strengths. This approach can end up having a greater impact on your employees' satisfaction in the workplace and overall productivity in the long run.

As a business leader, you can see where team members might be struggling, even with additional training. Being a responsible leader means looking at the bigger picture and making adjustments that benefit the business and your employees.

Regardless of whether you are leading, here are just a few of the practical ways responsibility impacts your leadership and how it can benefit both your family and business.

1. Acting Beyond Self-Interest

Responsibility is not about self-promotion; it's about dedicating your energy to help those around you without any personal gain. It is also about recognizing how helping others to thrive ultimately benefits your family, business, and community. While you might not always personally feel those benefits, knowing others are successful and thriving contributes to your joy and sense of purpose.

2. Practicing Empathy

To be responsible is to recognize that your decisions impact others. It requires putting yourself in someone else's shoes and acting with compassion and generosity. Acknowledging that helping others, even if it means making a sacrifice on your part, allows you to empower others and lead with mindfulness.

3. Embodying Humility

Humility in responsibility is thinking about how one can serve others rather than what one will gain. This mindset fosters trust and strengthens relationships. Humility also requires you to acknowledge where you might be limited and need to spend time learning to grow your understanding of others.

> **Reflection**: Ask yourself, "Am I serving to uplift others, or am I driven by personal motive?"

A responsible leader is focused not on what they need, but on how they can mindfully meet the needs of others. It contributes to growth as they identify areas where they need to expand their knowledge and experience, as well as how they can better deploy the strengths of others to benefit their family or business as a whole.

While the world sees responsibility as meeting your obligations and nothing more, leadership with purpose embraces responsibility as a way to help others thrive and build a solid foundation within the family, business, and community.

Why Responsibility Matters

1. **It Builds Trust and Reliability**

   Consistently taking responsibility, especially during challenges, establishes trust. People rely on responsible leaders to guide them with integrity and selflessness.

2. **It Creates Ripple Effects of Good**

   Acts of responsibility often inspire others to step up and to serve in a positive manner that will benefit a strong community.

3. **It Fosters Personal Growth**

   Responsibility challenges you to grow, adapt, and lead with purpose. Each act of service redefines your character and strengthens your fulfillment in life.

Examples of Responsibility in Action

Throughout this discussion of responsibility, I highlighted how practicing it can positively impact you in multiple personal and professional settings. As a parent, exercising responsibility for my children involves caring for their needs, including their emotional well-being, while also modeling values like respect and resilience that I want them to emulate. Each small, caring act reflects my commitment to our family's collective growth.

Being responsible means acknowledging my mistakes and taking steps to correct and make amends. The result is my children feel comfortable taking risks and making mistakes, knowing that they will learn and grow from the experience. On a spiritual level, every loving act in our home becomes a prayer of gratitude and devotion to the family unit, keeping them strong and grounded.

Practicing responsibility for my children also allows them to see me show up for my community meaningfully. A community leader who is responsible and humble takes the initiative to inspire others while also contributing and uplifting them, creating a sense of unity and a shared vision. When you are a responsible leader in this area, your children see how it benefits the community by making it stronger, more connected, and where everyone feels valued. As a parent of a child with autism, I must help to build a society and community where my child feels valued for her contribution, even if it does not look exactly like someone else's contribution.

Being responsible as a leader means highlighting the strengths and contributions of others, not trying to create a community that only values people who fit into predetermined boxes. Think of your community as a beautiful woven blanket. If you only use one or two colors, then it will lack vibrancy. You create a beautiful and practical work of art when you weave in different colors and patterns.

Our communities are like that blanket. They should be vibrant and reflect the contributions of all members, not just a few. Responsible leaders look to include more voices, thus strengthening the community as a whole.

Practical Strategies to Embrace Responsibility

As a business leader, I embrace strategies as a way to bring my vision for my business to life. In the same way, if you want to incorporate responsibility more fully into your leadership, practical strategies for doing so will assist you in achieving this goal. Here are a few of the practical strategies that benefited me as I embraced responsibility.

1. Lead by Example

Being a role model and taking accountability means reflecting responsibility through your actions. I am a role model for my children every day, so remembering that they are following my example helps me be more mindful of practicing responsibility in my words, decisions, and actions. This means showing up on time, taking accountability, and providing support to set the tone for those around you.

2. Empower Others

Delegating tasks while trusting the shared opinions of those around you and giving them validation fosters growth and confidence.

Guidance and encouragement provide individuals with a reason to feel valued and motivated for their future success.

3. Own the Outcome

Take responsibility for results, even when they fall short of expectations. Shift your focus from a negative outlook to a positive solution. This can foster resilience and growth in your personal life and professional life.

4. Create Safe Spaces

Encourage open dialogue and conversation. This allows others to share their opinions without the fear of judgment to build trust, strengthens relationships, and lays a concrete foundation for you to lead with purpose, while also being humble enough to know that you do not know everything.

Reflection and Action

Journal Prompt:

Reflect on a time when you hesitated to take responsibility. What held you back? How can you approach similar situations differently in the future?

Practical Step:

Identify one role—parent, leader, friend, or volunteer—where you can strengthen your sense of responsibility. Commit to one specific action that will create a positive impact.

Extended Exercise:

Responsibility Inventory

1. **List Your Roles**: Write down every role you hold (parent, colleague, mentor, friend, etc.).

2. **Evaluate Contributions**: Ask yourself, "Am I fully investing in these roles, or am I doing the bare minimum?"

3. **Set Goals**: Choose one specific action to elevate your contributions in each role.

4. **Revisit and Reflect**: Reassess your progress monthly to refine your approach and celebrate growth.

Conclusion: Commitments to Personal and Professional Responsibility

Responsibility is about serving with intention and compassion, using your skills to uplift others and create more meaningful change.

It is a commitment to navigating through your influences, talents, and resources to unlock your full potential and purpose while also helping others unlock their own potential and purpose. Whether you are leading as a parent, business owner, or member of the community, focus on serving responsibly and finding ways to assist others in contributing. Highlight strengths over weaknesses and find the lessons in mistakes and failures. Doing so will demonstrate a growth mindset, one that helps you to lead with intention, regardless of the circumstances.

As you continue reading, remember that responsibility builds on the foundation of accountability (personal ownership) and works alongside faithfulness (anchoring in purpose). These pillars create a framework for unshakable leadership that fosters growth, harmony, and everlasting impact.

Notes

_____

_____

_____

_____

_____

_____

_____

_____

_____

_____

_____

_____

_____

_____

_____

_____

_____

Chapter 4

Faithfulness—The Anchor of Leadership

*"Faithfulness is a pyramid of trust and loyalty;
it is a confidence in what we hope for and assurance
about what we do not see."*

– Pam Pabla

4

While many leaders prioritize results and utilize others' strengths effectively, most miss a key ingredient to leadership, which is faithfulness. A leader's ability to remain loyal to their principles, vision, and people forms the bedrock upon which trust and respect are built. It is about consistency, integrity, and a steadfast commitment to both personal values and organizational goals, even when faced with challenges or temptations to compromise.

At its core, faithfulness is about trust. A faithful leader demonstrates reliability and commitment, ensuring their actions align with their words.

Why Leaders Need Faithfulness

Faithfulness, in leadership, is an **unshakable** commitment to your purpose, vision, and values, even when the journey feels uncertain or the results are not immediate. While the outcome is important, it is also about remaining loyal to the process, and the larger mission you want to be served.

Faithfulness is a compass that guides leaders through ambiguity and adversity, ensuring they remain anchored in hope, clarity, and perseverance. Nurturing a family, managing a team, or leading a movement with faithfulness enables you to stay consistent in your efforts, knowing that every action contributes to a larger purpose.

At its core, leadership is about trust. A faithful leader demonstrates reliability and commitment, ensuring their actions align with their words. Consistency encourages others to follow, knowing that you will not waiver in your values. Trust fosters a positive organizational culture where collaboration and transparency thrive.

As a business owner, I have dealt with the realities of a changing economy. This means making decisions to keep my business profitable and thriving for myself and my employees. Remaining loyal to your employees during tough financial times instills a sense of security and loyalty that strengthens your relationship with others.

Faithfulness in leadership means remaining focused on your family's and business's long-term vision. This unwavering commitment drives progress and inspires those around you to stay engaged and motivated. Faithful leaders are not easily swayed by immediate pressures or fleeting trends, ensuring their decisions contribute to the enduring success of those they lead.

Part of being a faithful leader is acknowledging the truth honestly, even when the truth is difficult to face. Integrity and faithfulness go hand in hand—without one, the other cannot exist. Leaders faithful to their moral compass do not compromise their principles for convenience or personal gain. Their ethical foundation gives them the courage to make tough decisions, knowing their actions will always reflect the truth. Owning up to your mistakes, taking accountability, and working to rectify issues demonstrates immense faithfulness to the principle of honesty—earning the respect of others and fostering an environment where everyone feels safe to be transparent.

Leadership is full of setbacks, opposition, and moments of doubt. Faithfulness serves as a source of resilience during these times. A leader commits to their vision, team, and principles, thus equipping them to navigate adversity and helping them to provide a stabilizing force for those they lead.

Faithfulness is more than a desirable quality in leadership— it is essential. By building a foundation of trust and upholding integrity, you cultivate loyalty and dedication among those you lead. Faithfulness defines a leader's capacity to influence and inspire. In a constantly shifting world, a leader's unwavering faithfulness stands as a beacon, guiding others toward success.

Faithfulness as a Foundation for Leadership

My family is a vital part of my life, a source of support and love no matter what I am facing in my current circumstances. With the diagnosis of my child's autism, I had a new challenge: to help her reach her goals and empower her to achieve at her fullest potential. Autism was a gift and a challenge, one that helped me to look at the world with a different set of eyes.

It also helped me to tap into my faithfulness as a leader within my family. Instead of seeing autism as an impossible obstacle, I chose to see it as something we could use to benefit my child, increasing her resilience and empowering her to live according to her values and with purpose. Here are a few of the foundational principles of faithfulness that I modeled as a leader.

1. The Foundation of Strength

Faithfulness reassures leaders that every challenge, setback, or detour serves a higher purpose. Instead of viewing obstacles as failures, faithful leaders see them as opportunities for growth and refinement.

2. The Fuel for Perseverance

Faithfulness provides the emotional resilience to persevere through uncertainty. It reminds leaders that consistency often precedes the most meaningful triumphs.

Faithfulness in Leadership – The Spiritual Lens

Faithfulness in leadership is a cornerstone of effective and transformative guidance. Rooted in spiritual principles, faithfulness calls for you to exhibit leadership with unwavering commitment, integrity, and a deep sense of responsibility to those you serve. A faithful leader remains steadfast in your values, guided by divine wisdom and purpose.

Faithfulness in leadership means displaying an unwavering trust in God's plan. A leader who embodies faithfulness seeks divine guidance, ensuring their decisions align with God's will rather than personal ambition. The focus is on how you can serve versus being served. Faithfulness in leadership also mirrors the example of Christ, who displayed a willingness to serve in all areas of his life. True faithfulness requires humility and a willingness to prioritize the needs of others above self-interest. This mindset fosters trust and inspires those being led to cultivate the same spirit of service.

Leadership is not just a walk in the park but is full of internal and external challenges. Self-doubt can be one of those internal challenges, while a significant medical diagnosis can be one of those external challenges. Remaining steadfast in adversity calls for resilience, knowing that trials refine character and strengthen leadership capabilities.

Faithfulness in leadership creates a lasting impact as you build trust, foster a culture of ethical decision making, and inspire others to uphold the same principles. When leaders remain faithful to their calling, they thrive, cultivating an environment where righteousness and justice prevail. From a spiritual perspective, faithfulness is a deep commitment to serve others with integrity, humility, and perseverance. Leaders who embody these qualities reflect God's nature and set a powerful example for those they guide. Ultimately, a faithful leader's legacy is one of trust, righteousness, and a steadfast pursuit of God's purpose.

Defining Faithfulness in Leadership

Faithfulness in leadership can be defined as a steadfast dedication to principles of trust, integrity, and service, regardless of circumstances. It is the quality of remaining true to one's calling, responsibilities, and ethical beliefs even when faced with challenges. This faithfulness extends beyond personal gain and is deeply rooted in a commitment to serve others with humility and perseverance. Here are three ways that it manifests itself in leadership:

1. Self-Belief

Faithfulness begins with unwavering trust in one's abilities and experiences. It enables one to see failures as steppingstones to unlock one's full potential.

2. Belief in Others

Faithfulness extends to those you lead. You trust in their abilities, encourage growth, and provide the space for them to flourish.

3. Belief in a Higher Purpose

Faithfulness is grounded in the belief that your work contributes to a greater good, inspired by spirituality or a guiding compass, which leads to consistency and purpose.

Cultivating Faithfulness as a Leader

True faithfulness in leadership is about showing up with purpose and dedication to your mission and values. Cultivating faithfulness as a leader requires a commitment to accountability, responsibility, and integrity. Faithfulness can be strengthened through intentional practices that align your actions with your purpose:

1. Daily Practices

- **Morning Intentions**: Start each day with a positive affirmation about commitment to your vision and values.

- **Mindful Breathing**: When challenges arise, take a moment to pause, breathe, and realign.

2. Surround Yourself with Support

- **Like-Minded Individuals**: Build a network of mentors, peers, and communities that bring positivity and growth.

- **Collaborative Growth**: Share stories and experiences with others to remind yourself that faithfulness in leadership is a shared journey.

3. Learn from Setbacks

- **Reframing Failure**: View setbacks as opportunities to learn and grow, rather than reasons to give up.

- **Celebrate Small Wins**: Acknowledge progress, however small, to provide a sense of purpose and accomplishment.

Integrating Faithfulness with Accountability and Responsibility

Faithfulness strengthens and compliments the principles of accountability and responsibility because these three ideas are deeply intertwined. A faithful leader does not act solely based on personal desires but recognizes their duty to God, their team, and their community. Accountability means being answerable for one's actions and decisions, ensuring that integrity and ethical principles guide their leadership. As a leader, you must acknowledge your role in stewarding your position with wisdom and humility.

On the other hand, responsibility entails actively fulfilling one's duties with diligence and care. A faithful leader understands that their influence comes with expectations and a willingness to shepherd their duties with unwavering commitment. When faithfulness integrates with accountability and responsibility, leadership becomes a powerful force for positive transformation, fostering trust and stability. As a leader, you must own your decisions while trusting your efforts align with a greater purpose. Serving others with consistent dedication, every act of leadership contributes to a larger narrative of growth and transformation.

Reflection and Action

Journal Prompt:

Reflect on a challenge where your perseverance wavered. How might faithfulness have helped you approach it differently? What steps can you take now to cultivate faithfulness in similar situations?

Practical Step:

1. Identify an area in your life where faithfulness feels lacking—family, work, or personal growth.

2. Write down two actions you can take daily to stay committed to that area, even when progress feels slow.

3. Share your commitment with a trusted friend or mentor who can offer encouragement.

Conclusion: The Power of Faithfulness

Unshakable leadership is built on faithfulness.

It transforms obstacles into opportunities, ensuring that your efforts contribute to meaningful growth, both for yourself and those you lead. Faithfulness is shown through loyalty, unwavering commitments, honesty, and reliability.

As you integrate **faithfulness** with **accountability** and **responsibility**, you build a leadership framework that is resilient, intentional, and impactful. In the chapters ahead, we will explore how mindset, positivity, and the power of thoughts enhance this foundation, empowering you to lead with **unshakable** confidence.

Notes

_____

_____

_____

_____

_____

_____

_____

_____

_____

_____

_____

_____

_____

_____

_____

Part Three

Chapter 5

Integrating the Three Pillars– Accountability, Responsibility, and Faithfulness

"Success is the sum of consistent small efforts,
which are built by integrating or incorporating accountability,
responsibility, and faithfulness."
—Pam Pabla

5

Throughout the last few chapters, I focused on the importance of accountability, responsibility, and faithfulness as integral parts of creating purposeful leadership and modeling it for others. As I explored leadership and the lessons from my child's experiences and development, it showed me that to effectively integrate these three things, a leader must be able to embody several key principles.

First, they require you as a leader to remain truthful and principled. A leader cultivates trust and reliability by making ethical decisions and standing firm in righteousness. Accountability thrives in an environment where leaders willingly accept feedback and make necessary improvements. A faithful leader invites guidance from both God and those they serve.

Responsibility means acknowledging both successes and failures. Leaders who take ownership of their actions foster a culture of growth and learning while still fulfilling their obligations. These leaders who consistently demonstrate faithfulness, accountability, and responsibility build enduring relationships and inspire those around them to uphold the same values.

Why Integration Matters

Leadership is about combining essential qualities such as accountability, responsibility, **and faithfulness** to create a unified and transformative approach. These pillars are not just individual traits; they are interconnected principles that, when integrated, elevate leadership from task management to meaningful influence.

So far, you've explored the core pillars individually:

1. **Accountability** – Taking ownership of your decisions, whether right or wrong, even amid uncertainty and pressure.

2. **Responsibility** – Leading with integrity to ensure that your actions fulfill your tasks and choices for the best interest of yourself and others.

3. **Faithfulness** – Trusting in a vision beyond the physical realm allows hope and perseverance to guide you through life.

Accountability ensures transparency and ownership of your goals. **Responsibility** expands our duties to uplift others. **Faithfulness** infuses both with perseverance and hope, ensuring you remain steady in the face of uncertainty. Together, they form the tripod upon which **unshakable** leadership stands for. These three pillars serve a unique purpose.

The Alliance of the Three Pillars

While each of the core pillars we discussed plays its part in building leadership that serves and motivates others, it is important to understand how they integrate to build unshakable leadership. My focus here is giving you practical ways to utilize these core pillars in all aspects of your life, while creating a foundation that allows everyone in your family and business to thrive.

1. Accountability + Responsibility

When combined, accountability and responsibility create a culture of trust, support, and collaboration. Leaders who embody both principles foster environments where people feel valued and inspired to contribute.

- **Insight**: Consider a family that practices both accountability and responsibility. Parents are transparent about finances, household expectations, and personal growth. Children, in turn, learn the importance of taking responsibility for their own chores, studies, and relationships. The result is a harmonious family dynamic where everyone thrives.

2. Accountability + Faithfulness

This combination strengthens resilience. Accountability ensures alignment with goals, and faithfulness provides the courage to navigate setbacks and uncertainties.

- **Insight**: An entrepreneur launching a new product might face market unpredictability, and accountability ensures that they follow their business plan and adjust as needed. Faithfulness gives them the confidence to persist, knowing their efforts align with a greater purpose and will be rewarded.

3. Responsibility + Faithfulness

When faithfulness guides responsibility, leaders serve with compassion, dedication, and patience. Even when immediate results are not visible, faithfulness affirms that every act of service holds meaning.

- **Insight**: A volunteer teacher in an underserved community pours energy into after-school programs. Progress is gradual, but their faithfulness assures them that the seeds of knowledge planted today will give them hope for tomorrow's successes.

The Power of Integration

Let's revisit my story from Chapter 1 when I received my child's autism diagnosis. Here is how I integrated each of these aspects of leadership to the benefit of my child and my business.

1. **Accountability**: I took ownership of my child's developmental journey, learning about therapies, milestones, and resources. I held myself accountable for creating opportunities for growth and seeking solutions instead of waiting for others to provide these opportunities.

2. **Responsibility**: My efforts extended beyond my child. I built a network of supportive professionals, friends, and family members, creating a community of understanding and compassion that supported me and my child.

3. **Faithfulness**: I trusted that every intervention, therapy session, and moment of encouragement was part of a larger

plan for my child's unique potential, thus allowing me to prioritize her needs while highlighting the importance of being willing to serve in a variety of circumstances.

By integrating these three core pillars, I transformed heartbreak into purpose. The progress in my child's communication skills, stronger family bonds, and a ripple effect of hope and encouragement motivate other parents facing similar challenges.

Reflection and Action

Journal Prompt:

Reflect on an area of your life where the three pillars could bring balance. Which pillar do you need to strengthen, and how can you integrate it into your daily leadership?

Action Step:

Choose one specific project—personal, family, or professional. Create a plan to incorporate all three pillars this week:

- **Accountability:** Set measurable goals.

- **Responsibility:** Identify who benefits and how to serve them better.

- **Faithfulness:** Anchor your actions in trust that progress will unfold.

Conclusion: A Strong Foundation for
Unshakable Leadership

The integration of **accountability, responsibility, and faithfulness** creates a leadership framework that is resilient, compassionate, and purposeful. Accountability ensures honesty; responsibility drives engagement; and faithfulness reinforces commitment. These pillars form a foundation for personal growth, collective impact, and **unshakable** perseverance.

By mastering this practice, you elevate your leadership in transformational ways. As you continue to the next chapters on **mindset, positivity**, and the **power of thoughts,** you'll learn how these principles complement the core pillars, helping you lead with clarity, optimism, and purpose, regardless of the challenges in life.

Notes

_____

_____

_____

_____

_____

_____

_____

_____

_____

_____

_____

_____

_____

_____

_____

Chapter 6

The Secret Formula for Success

"Having a clear vision allows you to support your goals for a purposeful life."
—Pam Pabla

6

Success is commonly defined as the achievement of a desired outcome or goal. According to Merriam-Webster, it encompasses "a favorable or desired outcome." The Cambridge Dictionary describes it as the "achieving of the results wanted or hoped for."

While these definitions help us to understand what the word might mean, the interpretation of success can vary greatly based upon individual values and contexts. While some may view success in terms of material accomplishments, others might define it through personal growth, fulfillment, or their positive impact on others. Spiritually, success is often aligned with living according to one's faith and principles, emphasizing integrity, service, and inner peace over external achievements.

Success

The true meaning of success lies in harmonizing your purpose, values, and actions to craft a meaningful life and lead with grace and humility. It's about fostering growth in yourself and others while contributing to something greater. The journey of success is as important as the destination. It is about achieving inner peace that brings satisfaction to one's life.

Why Success Needs a Deeper Definition

Success often requires a deeper definition because traditional metrics, including how much wealth you have or your social status, may not fully capture fulfillment and purpose. Relying solely on external achievements can lead to a sense of emptiness or a continuous pursuit of more, without ever attaining genuine satisfaction. By exploring a more comprehensive understanding of success, you can align your goals with your values to build a meaningful and contented life. This broader perspective acknowledges that true success encompasses personal growth, your mental, emotional and physical well-being, and the positive impact you have on others, rather than just increasing your net worth or social status.

Many people compare success with external and materialistic wins. But what happens when the applause fades, adversity strikes, or when reality kicks in? Superficial success cannot sustain you through the challenges that life throws your way.

A Higher Calling: Success must reflect the harmony between **accountability**, **responsibility**, and **faithfulness**. These pillars create a foundation that outshines momentary wins. When combined, they assist you in leading others with empathy, respect, and grace, acknowledging that we are all learning and growing throughout this life.

Personal and Collective Dimensions

True success enriches both your own life and the lives of others. As a leader that serves others instead of waiting to be served, you look for ways to empower others and help them to build their leadership skills. Take a moment and reflect on someone's example that profoundly impacted your life. What did they do that you want to emulate? How did they navigate disappointments or wins? Did they pull others up along the way, or seek to build themselves up by bringing others down?

- **In a family**: Success might mean raising compassionate children, fostering open communication, and supporting one another through wins and challenges.

- **In a workplace**: Success could mean creating a culture of respect, innovation, and collaboration where everyone feels empowered to thrive together.

The Four Cornerstones of Meaningful Success

The "secret formula" for success intertwines four foundational elements:

1. **Vision**: A clear, heartfelt direction that inspires action.

2. **Integrity**: Living in alignment with your core values, no matter the circumstances.

3. **Resilience**: Turning trials into steppingstones for growth.

4. **Faithfulness in the Process**: Trusting that your efforts contribute to a greater design, even when progress feels slow.

Diving Deeper into Four Cornerstones

1. Vision: Seeing Beyond the Present

Vision is the spark that ignites meaningful action. It is the "why" behind your efforts, the reason you get out of bed each morning. A clear vision inspires both you and those around you to persevere, even when the road ahead is uncertain.

- **Spiritual Perspective**

  A vision rooted in universal values such as compassion, justice, or unity transcends personal gain. It reminds you that every milestone serves a larger picture, connecting you to the universe.

2. Integrity: Living Your Values Daily

Integrity is the glue that holds leadership together. It's the commitment to align your words and actions with your values, even when no one is watching.

- **Spiritual Perspective**

  Integrity is akin to "walking in truth." Your inner and outer actions need to be aligned to be true to yourself and show the divine power that you are genuine, which brings you peace of mind.

3. Resilience: Turning Trials into Triumphs

Resilience is not only about enduring hardships; it is about growing stronger. Resilient leaders view setbacks as opportunities to learn, adapt, and emerge for a better future.

- **Spiritual Perspective**

  Unintentional mistakes cultivate empathy and humility through the challenges that are not under your control.

4. Faithfulness in the Process: Trust the Timing

Even with a clear vision, integrity and resilience often unfolds on its own. Faithfulness in the process assures you that every effort contributes to a greater plan on its own timing.

- **Spiritual Perspective**

  In life we are not in control of "when" or "how" things happen, but we must have faith in the divine, to reveal the answers when the timing is right or when we are ready.

Reflection and Action

Journal Prompt:

What does success mean to you? How does it align with your values, goals, and sense of purpose? Reflect on how vision, integrity, resilience, and faithfulness currently play a role in your life—and where there's room for growth.

Action Step:

1. Identify a project or goal you're currently working on.

2. Evaluate how well it aligns with each cornerstone:

   - **Vision**: Is your "why" clear?

   - **Integrity**: Are your actions aligned with your values?

- **Resilience**: Are you committed to adapting and learning from challenges?
- **Faithfulness**: Do you trust the process, even when results are slow?

3. Adjust your approach to strengthen any missing elements.

Conclusion:

The world's standards do not define success; it is about living a life of purpose, consistency, and impact. The secret formula for success—**vision, integrity, resilience, and faithfulness**—intertwines with the core pillars of **accountability, responsibility, and faithfulness**. This equips you to lead with clarity, hope, and perseverance for your future.

When you integrate these principles into your daily life, you create a legacy of meaningful growth that touches everyone you lead and serve. As you move forward into the next chapters on **mindset, positivity, and the power of thoughts**, you will learn how to deepen this framework, unlocking the full potential of **unshakable** leadership.

Notes

Chapter 7

Intentional Leadership

"Intentional leadership is leading with a good heart, intent, and a clear mindset, knowing you are doing the right things."
—Pam Pabla

7

What Is Intentional Leadership?

Intentional leadership is about leading and living with purpose. It is about proactively aligning your actions, decisions, and attitudes with your core values and vision rather than reacting to circumstances as they arise. Unlike reactive leadership, where actions are driven by circumstances or pressure, intentional leaders focus on long-term goals and build a positive, impactful culture.

Intentional leadership is unshakeable in today's fast-paced world, where distractions are endless and demands relentless. It is the ability to remain anchored, deliberate, and purpose-driven in every interaction.

Applying intentional leadership means practicing deliberate actions to inspire and guide others effectively. Start with a clear vision and purpose that aligns with your values and organizational goals. Share this vision with those you lead, so everyone understands the "why" behind their efforts. As an intentional leader, be a role model for the values and behaviors you want to see. Consistency in your actions builds trust and credibility.

Connect regularly with those you lead, offering constructive feedback where necessary. Intentional communication fosters a sense of belonging and alignment. Encourage autonomy and provide growth opportunities. Recognize others' strengths and delegate tasks that align with their talents. No matter what, stay resilient and adaptable. Challenges are inevitable, so you need to respond to them in a way that aligns with your values and vision. Doing so will inspire those under your leadership to stay focused and flexible, regardless of the changing circumstances.

Key Attributes of Intentional Leaders

Being an intentional leader involves several attributes that help them to lead with purpose and vision. Let's dive into what each of those is and how they impact your leadership.

1. Clarity of Purpose

They know their rational behind their actions and align their decisions daily with that rational, as well as their values, whether they're leading a company, nurturing a family, or serving their community.

- **Spiritual Perspective**: Many intentional leaders view their work as part of a divine calling, connecting each action to a higher purpose.

2. Cultivation of Self-Awareness

They regularly reflect on how well their actions match their beliefs and goals.

- **Spiritual Perspective:** An intentional leader might keep a journal and connect with divine power for guidance.

3. Deliberate Action

They prioritize quality over quantity, focusing their energy on tasks and decisions that drive meaningful progress.

Why Intentional Leadership Matters

Intentional leadership matters because it creates a foundation for meaningful impact and lasting success, both personally and professionally. Leaders with intention make decisions that foster consistency and trust. By focusing on empathy and understanding, intentional leaders inspire collaboration and individual growth, which boosts morale and productivity.

When times are challenging, either due to the industry or larger economic shifts, intentional leadership maintains the focus, enabling teams to adapt without losing sight of long-term goals. Opting for intentional leadership helps you to set the tone and culture of your home or workplace, establishing a culture of transparency, respect, and shared purpose. Here are a few of the other practical ways intentional leadership impacts those around you.

1. Reduces Burnout and Chaos

Leaders who lack intention often fall victim to the whirlwind of daily tasks, losing themselves and their teams in busy work. Intentional leaders focus on long-term goals, reducing stress and preserving energy for what truly matters.

2. Promotes Alignment and Trust

People thrive under leaders who make deliberate, thoughtful choices. By communicating purpose and rationale, intentional leaders foster trust and loyalty within their teams, families, or communities.

3. Strengthens Moral and Spirituality

Intentional leaders consult their values, ethics, and morals, before making decisions, ensuring their actions are aligned with their beliefs. This fosters ethical clarity and a sense of peace.

- **Spiritual Perspective**: Such leaders see their work as part of a larger, sacred story. This perspective helps them navigate both triumphs and trials with grace.

Core Attributes of Intentional Leadership

Ultimately, intentional leadership isn't just about achieving goals; it is about creating a ripple effect that benefits people, organizations, and communities. By working to advocate for my child, I helped to shape the educational landscape for her and other children with autism. It also helped me to see that I can create meaningful change for those in my family and in my business, by how I choose to carry myself in these areas. Intentional leadership is not necessarily loud but can work behind the scenes to create meaningful change.

How can you implement intentional leadership? It starts with these core attributes, which can assist you in finding clarity and purpose.

1. Clarity of Purpose

Intentional leaders start with a clear mission. They know what they're working toward and use this clarity as their guiding star.

- **Defining Your Mission**: Take time to articulate a concise, meaningful purpose that resonates with your values.

- **Spiritual Perspective**: A purpose rooted in values like compassion or justice ties your efforts to universal principles, making every step meaningful.

2. Consistent Reflection

Intentional leaders carve out time for regular self-assessment to ensure their actions remain aligned with their vision.

- **Check-Ins**: Daily journaling or weekly discussions help track progress, celebrate wins, and realign when needed.

3. Effective Communication

Transparency is a hallmark of intentional leadership. Leaders who openly share their rationale build trust and invite collaboration.

- **Empathetic Listening**: Intentional leaders actively seek feedback, ensuring that everyone feels heard and valued.

4. Purposeful Action

Intentional leaders focus on tasks that align with their values and vision, avoiding the trap of spreading themselves too thin.

- **Calm Yet Decisive**: They pause to reflect before acting, responding thoughtfully rather than reacting impulsively.

Intentional Leadership in Daily Life

1. **At Home**: A parent sets the intention to create a supportive home environment where children feel heard and loved.

   • **Actions**: Thoughtfully managing discipline, allocating chores, and prioritizing quality family time.

   • **Result**: Children grow up with a sense of security and purpose, mirroring the parent's intentional approach in their own lives.

2. **In the Workplace**: A leader focuses on a monthly theme, such as "innovation through collaboration," structuring meetings and brainstorming sessions to reflect this intention.

   • **Outcome**: Team members see their routine tasks as part of a larger vision, boosting morale and creativity.

3. **In Community Service**: Volunteers at a soup kitchen begin each shift with a reflection on the dignity of those they serve.

   • **Reward**: Recipients feel genuine care, creating a ripple effect of positivity, gratitude, and often, a desire to give back.

Bridging Intentional Leadership with Accountability, Responsibility, and Faithfulness

1. **Accountability and Intention**

   Intentional leaders hold themselves accountable for aligning their goals and actions with their values.

2. **Responsibility and Intention**

   Responsibility adds a grounded mindset to intentional leadership, emphasizing the impact of your choices on others.

3. **Faithfulness and Intention**

   Faithfulness infuses intention with hope and resilience, enabling leaders to trust in the process even when results are slow.

Overcoming Common Obstacles to Intentional Leadership

Overcoming obstacles to intentional leadership requires clarity, resilience, and a willingness to adapt. To find the right solution for your obstacle, you must understand the specific challenges, whether they are a lack of trust, misaligned goals, or resistance to change. Doing so allows you to address issues systematically rather than reactively.

Stick to your core values and vision, even in difficult situations. A solid foundation of purpose helps guide decision making and keep those you lead aligned in their mindset and actions. Managing emotions, both yours and others, is essential for navigating conflict or resistance. Practice empathy, patience, and self-awareness to lead effectively through challenges.

Transparency also fosters trust. When you are transparent about the obstacles and welcome input from others to craft the solution, you create resolutions collaboratively, while also fostering an environment where obstacles are identified and addressed early on.

Flexibility is key to overcoming obstacles. Rigid leadership does not allow for adaptability to changing circumstances. Whether it is adjusting strategies or exploring creative solutions, adaptability ensures you and your business overcome hurdles without losing sight of your goals and vision.

From Obstacles to Successful Leadership

Struggling to lead with intention? Here are three situations and solutions to help you lead more effectively.

1. **Distractions and Overcommitment**

   - **Issue**: Juggling too many tasks can distract you from your vision.

   - **Solution**: Evaluate tasks regularly and eliminate those that do not align with your core vision. Focus on quality, not quantity.

2. **Emotional Reactivity**

   - **Issue**: High stress can lead to hasty and impulsive decisions, leading to misaligned outcomes.

- **Solution**: Develop emotional intelligence by pausing for reflection or seeking divine guidance before responding to challenges.

3. **Resistance from Others**

- **Issue**: Colleagues or family members may resist your intentional approach, especially if they are accustomed to chaos.

- **Solution**: Demonstrate consistency and patience. Over time, your thoughtful leadership will build trust and influence.

Reflection and Action

Journal Prompt:

What area of your life feels the most chaotic or reactive? What intentional steps can you take to bring greater purpose and alignment to that area?

Action Step:

Write a leadership intention for the week (e.g., "I will focus on fostering collaboration within my team").

Schedule daily check-ins to track progress and make adjustments as needed.

Invite feedback from a trusted colleague, friend, or family member to keep yourself accountable.

Extended Exercise: One Intentional Day

Goal: Experience the power of intentional leadership by dedicating one full day to mindful choices.

1. **Morning Reflection**: Identify a guiding value for the day (e.g., empathy, focus, or gratitude).

2. **Mid-day Check-In**: Reflect on whether your actions and interactions honor that value. Adjust if necessary.

3. **Evening Debrief**: Celebrate small wins and identify areas for improvement. Write down one lesson to carry forward into the next day.

Conclusion

Intentional leadership is about leading with purpose, clarity, and compassion. By aligning your actions with your values and vision, you inspire trust, foster growth, and create lasting impact.

As you continue to enhance your leadership, the principles of **accountability, responsibility,** and **faithfulness** will strengthen your intentionality, helping you stay grounded and resilient. In the upcoming chapters, we will continue to discuss mindset, positivity, and the power of thoughts to help you discover how inner alignment complements outward purpose, shaping you into an **unshakable** leader capable of transforming both lives and legacies.

Notes

_____

_____

_____

_____

_____

_____

_____

_____

_____

_____

_____

_____

_____

_____

_____

_____

Chapter 8

Embracing the Breakdown Before the Breakthrough

"Breakthrough comes after the biggest breakdown in life, so do not give up; keep moving forward."
—Pam Pabla

8

Introduction:
The Hidden Gift in Challenges

Breakdowns are inevitable in life. They can take the form of a failed business project, a family disagreement, or even a personal crisis of self-doubt. While such moments often feel like dead ends, they are, in reality, critical junctures—places where old ways of thinking or operating no longer serve us. Breakdowns force us to pause, reflect, and reset.

The most transformative leaders, parents, and innovators understand that breakdowns are not the end of the story. In fact, they often mark the beginning of something extraordinary: the breakthrough.

A breakdown disrupts your status quo. It may highlight weaknesses, expose blind spots, or demand changes that you've avoided. But when approached with the pillars of **accountability, responsibility, and faithfulness**, these moments become the fertile ground for profound growth, innovation, and deeper alignment with purpose.

Why Breakdowns Precede Breakthroughs

1. Breakdowns are Catalysts for Innovation

When familiar methods fail, you're forced to think outside the box. Breakdowns compel creativity and experimentation, pushing you toward solutions you might never have considered otherwise.

- **Professional Example**: A nonprofit faces a funding crisis, threatening its mission. The challenge forces the team to innovate, launching creative crowdfunding campaigns and forming partnerships with local businesses. These efforts not only solve the funding problem but also expand the nonprofit's reach and impact.

2. Breakdowns Confront Blind Spots

Breakdowns often expose areas we've overlooked—whether it's an unhealthy work dynamic, outdated practices, or personal habits holding us back. Facing these blind spots is the first step toward growth.

- **Practical Benefit**: Leaders who confront blind spots build stronger, more harmonious teams. Families that address miscommunication foster deeper understanding and unity.

3. Breakdowns Deepen Spiritual Resilience

Spiritually, breakdowns are invitations to grow in faithfulness and humility. They challenge us to surrender control and trust in a higher purpose.

- **Illustration**: A business owner whose venture collapses may discover a new calling—one that aligns more deeply with their values and brings greater fulfillment.

Core Principles for Embracing Breakdowns

Embracing breakdowns as opportunities for breakthroughs requires a mindset shift and a clear strategy. Recognize that breakdowns are a natural part of the growth process and lead to progress. Accept them without judgment, because resistance only magnifies their impact.

Reflect deeply on the cause of the breakdown. Understand the emotions, behaviors, and decisions that may have led to the situation. Each challenge carries insights that can lead to personal or professional breakthroughs. Building inner strength by staying calm and optimistic, along with resilience, allows you to navigate setbacks and emerge stronger.

Building the right mindset means shifting your perspective from dwelling on the problem to exploring creative solutions. Don't hesitate to seek peers, mentors, or other support. Breakthroughs often come from shared ideas and collective effort.

It is essential to recognize that breakdowns often signal a need for change. The status quo is no longer working. Embrace the discomfort and commit to growing beyond your current limitations. Breakdowns, although challenging, serve as a catalyst for meaningful transformation. How can you process them more effectively?

1. Acknowledge Emotional Turbulence

Breakdowns often stir emotions like frustration, fear, or grief. While leaders may feel pressure to stay stoic, it's essential to acknowledge and process these emotions.

- **Healthy Processing**: Journaling, talking to a mentor, or practicing mindfulness can help you move through emotional turbulence without becoming overwhelmed.

2. Take Accountability and Responsibility

- **Accountability**: Own your role in the situation. What decisions or actions contributed to the breakdown? This self-reflection is the foundation for meaningful change.

- **Responsibility**: Recognize the ripple effects on others and take proactive steps to support those impacted. Transparent communication and a willingness to collaborate foster trust and shared solutions.

3. Integrate Faithfulness into the Storm

Faithfulness reminds us that challenges are temporary and often purposeful. You can weather the storm with hope and resilience by staying anchored in your higher vision.

- **Spiritual Practice**: Reflect on how this breakdown might be guiding you toward a better path. Trust that every step serves a greater purpose even when progress seems invisible.

4. Prepare for the Rebuild

The real transformation happens when you shift your focus from the breakdown itself to what comes next. What lessons have you learned? What needs to change to prevent future breakdowns?

- **Example**: A family experiencing financial strain might use this moment to reevaluate spending habits, set clearer goals, and create a healthier relationship with money.

Breakdowns in Action: Real-Life Snapshots

1. Winston Churchill: A Political Comeback

Churchill faced repeated political failures early in his career, including being blamed for disastrous decisions during World War I. Rather than retreat, he used these failures to refine his leadership. When WWII began, his resilience, vision, and courage made him one of history's most iconic leaders.

2. Business Turnaround

A small business facing bankruptcy due to poor management uses the crisis to overhaul operations, streamline processes, and refocus on customer relationships. Within a year, the business not only recovers but thrives, strengthened by lessons learned during the breakdown.

3. A Parent's Journey

A parent struggles to connect with their teenage child, leading to frequent conflicts. Instead of giving up, the parent seeks counseling, learns active listening skills, and adjusts their approach to communication. Over time, the relationship transforms, building trust and mutual respect.

Navigating the Breakdown to Breakthrough Process

1. Recognize Early Signs

Breakdowns don't usually happen overnight. Stress, declining morale, or repeated mistakes often signal deeper issues. Pay attention to these warning signs and address them proactively.

2. Engage in Honest Dialogue

Transparency is key. Open conversations with your team, family, or mentors foster understanding and collective problem solving. Be an active listener, not judging the input of others, so you can benefit from their perspective.

3. Plan the Rebuild

Breakdowns demand thoughtful solutions. Develop a clear action plan incorporating lessons learned, setting measurable goals, and engaging everyone involved. Doing so allows you to be accountable to yourself and others, while also distributing responsibility in a way that lightens everyone's load.

- **Example**: A project manager holds a retrospective meeting after a missed deadline, using feedback to adjust workflows and prevent future delays.

4. Invite Faith and Hope

Let go of what no longer serves you, trusting that the process of rebuilding will lead to something better. Affirm daily that challenges are opportunities in disguise.

Reflection and Action

Journal Prompt:

Think about a recent breakdown in your life—whether personal, professional, or relational. Ask yourself:

- What lessons did this situation reveal?

- How can I use this experience to create meaningful change?

Action Step:

1. Write down three potential breakthroughs that could arise from your current challenge.

2. For each, list one immediate step to move forward. Examples: having a heart-to-heart conversation, seeking training, or dedicating time to reflective prayer or meditation.

Extended Exercise: Your Breakthrough Blueprint

Goal: Transform a breakdown into a breakthrough with a structured plan.

3. **Identify the Breakdown**

   - Define the issue. What's not working? What's causing stress or disruption?

4. **Analyze Contributing Factors**

   - Reflect honestly on your role. What habits, decisions, or blind spots contributed to this situation?

5. **Visualize the Breakthrough**

- Imagine the ideal outcome. How would resolution look and feel?

6. **Design the Action Map**

- Break your vision into actionable steps. Assign responsibilities, set deadlines, and incorporate regular check-ins to track progress.

7. **Monitor, Adjust, and Celebrate**

- Celebrate small wins along the way. Recognize that progress is often nonlinear but always meaningful.

Conclusion: Commitment to the Process

Breakdowns, though painful, are not the end—they are invitations to grow. They push us out of our comfort zones, illuminate areas for improvement, and set the stage for breakthroughs that wouldn't otherwise be possible.

By embracing these moments with **accountability** (taking ownership), **responsibility** (serving those impacted), and **faithfulness** (trusting the process), you can transform crises into steppingstones for more tremendous success and fulfillment.

As we move into the next chapters on **mindset, positivity, and the power of thoughts**, you'll discover how to strengthen your inner dialogue and harness optimism to navigate even the most challenging breakdowns. Each breakdown has the potential to become your most potent breakthrough—if you choose to see it that way.

Notes

_____

_____

_____

_____

_____

_____

_____

_____

_____

_____

_____

_____

_____

_____

_____

Part Four

Chapter 9

The Mindset of an Unshakable Leader

"An unshakable leader is one who has a powerful and stable mindset to achieve goals in life."
—Pam Pabla

9

Introduction:
The Power of Mindset

An unshakable mindset is the foundation of exceptional leadership. The silent, steady voice guides you during uncertainty, fuels resilience during challenges, and anchors you in hope when progress feels distant. A leader's mindset is contagious—spreading energy, optimism, or doubt to those they lead.

While skills and strategies can be taught, mindsets are cultivated. It is a choice to approach every moment with faith, accountability, and the belief that growth is always possible. You have the power to shape your mindset with conscious effort in terms of what you focus your thoughts on and the habits you cultivate. As a leader, your choices become a model for those around you, whether you formally lead them or not.

With my child's journey, my mindset helped set the tone for them. If my mindset was positive and growth-oriented, then it was easier for them to see failures and setbacks as learning opportunities. For me, that mindset taught me how to view setbacks not as an expression of my worth but as a chance for me to expand my knowledge and creativity.

The Ripple Effect of a Leader's Mindset

A motivated leader inspires others by demonstrating commitment, resilience, and passion. Motivated leaders also lead by example, creating a ripple effect that encourages others to stay focused and energized. It was motivating to my family, especially my child, when I didn't focus on the diagnosis as a negative but as a positive with unique benefits.

As a leader, when things go wrong, you can energize those you lead by focusing on what is going right and what benefits you can take away from the experience. When something breaks, it exposes weaknesses that you can then address to make a system or process stronger. As a leader, your mindset and attitude toward these weaknesses or broken moments sets the tone for those who you are accountable for and to.

Motivation tends to flow naturally when your mindset is aligned with growth and positivity. A leader's mindset is like a pebble dropped into still water—its influence ripples far and wide. A positive, growth-oriented mindset sets the tone and shapes the overall culture of your family or business, while shaping the culture, productivity, and even long-term success.

For example, a leader who values innovation and embraces failure as a learning opportunity creates a ripple of creativity and resilience throughout their business. Leaders who demonstrate empathy foster trust, collaboration, and loyalty, thus fabricating a culture based upon making people feel valued and motivated.

Conversely, a negative or fixed mindset can stifle innovation and discourage risk-taking, spreading fear or complacency. Leaders cast long shadows, and their mindsets either inspire people to strive for greatness or limit their potential.

What's remarkable is how those ripples extend beyond those in your immediate circle. Your employees carry those lessons and attitudes into their networks and future roles, multiplying the impact of your mindset over time.

1. Influence on Morale

A leader with an empowering mindset uplifts others, creating an environment where challenges are viewed as opportunities, and individuals feel safe to take risks.

- **Example**: A leader facing a budget cut encourages those around them by saying, "This gives us a chance to innovate and redefine how we allocate resources. Let's find creative solutions."

2. Resilience in Adversity

An unshakable mindset doesn't crumble under pressure. Instead, it sees setbacks as temporary and opportunities for growth as constant.

- **Illustration**: Think of an athlete who loses a championship but uses the experience to train harder, refine techniques, and come back stronger the next season.

3. Inspires Faith in Others

When leaders trust in the process and maintain a growth mindset, they inspire confidence in their vision, encouraging those around them to believe in their shared mission.

Clearly, there are various benefits to having this type of mindset, one of which is focused on building up those around you and setting an example to keep them moving forward, aligned with your vision for your business. As a leader, developing a positive leader mindset involves deliberate practice and self-reflection.

Start shifting your mindset by regularly reflecting on your thoughts and behaviors to understand how they impact others. Seek feedback from colleagues to gain a balanced perspective of your choices and actions and identify areas where you might need to be more conscious of how you think and speak.

How do you view challenges? Do you see them as something you have to struggle through, bringing a negative attitude and assumption that the worst is happening? A positive growth mindset is different from a negative mindset in that a growth mindset sees challenges as a chance to grow, learn, and tap into your team's creativity. Instead of seeing them as the worst, leaders with a growth mindset see challenges as a way to help them thrive.

Personally, having to advocate for my child taught me the importance of empathy in leadership. Instead of jumping to conclusions or starting to assign blame without all the facts, I focus on active listening without interruption or judgment. To gain a different perspective, I take what they have shared and try to put myself in their position. Doing so helps me not only understand the needs of my child but also the needs of those I lead professionally. Empathy, regardless of the situation, helps you to understand the underlying causes. Knowing those causes can assist you in finding the best solutions, the ones with lasting impact, instead of continuing to pick band-aid solutions that only work temporarily. A growth mindset supports digging deeper to understand versus placing blame. Accountable leaders also acknowledge how their lack of understanding might have played a role in the current situation and opt to focus on how they can deepen their knowledge of the problem and make the appropriate corrections.

Another benefit of shifting your mindset is how it opens up your vision to better comprehend all the aspects of a challenge. One thing I have recognized is that negativity in our thinking breeds close-mindedness. When you are close-minded, it is as if you lose the ability to see the bigger picture or understand everything going on because your vision is now extremely narrow.

Humility is essential to leading with faithfulness and integrity. Growth mindsets are based on the idea that you don't know everything and are humble enough to prioritize the needs of your family and business. The result is a willingness to listen, learn, and support the growth of those around you.

Characteristics of an Unshakable Mindset

1. **Growth Orientation**

   - **Key Principle**: Every challenge is an opportunity to learn. A growth mindset focuses on progress, not perfection.

Action Step: After each setback, ask yourself, *"What is this teaching me, and how can I use it to improve?"*

2. Emotional Regulation

Leaders with a strong mindset know their emotions influence those they lead. They don't suppress feelings but manage them constructively.

- **Exercise**: When faced with a triggering situation, take 30 seconds to pause, breathe deeply, and shift from reaction to intentional response.

3. Faith-Driven Vision

An unshakable leader believes in a purpose greater than themselves, allowing them to stay focused even when results aren't immediately visible.

- **Reflection Prompt**: What bigger purpose fuels your work, and how does it guide your decisions?

Mindset Practices to Elevate Leadership

Clearly, having a growth mindset—open to the ideas of others—can give you the ability to tap into the experience and skills of those you lead. However, the challenges of running a business and managing a family can be overwhelming at times. Maintaining your growth mindset during these periods takes conscious effort on your part.

One of the ways that I do this is through my daily routine. By consciously setting my mindset for the day, I am putting myself in the right position to deal with challenges as the type of leader I want to be, one focused on integrity, accountability, responsibility, and faithfulness. Here are some practical exercises you can utilize as part of your routine to assist you in fostering and maintaining a mindset that compliments your leadership, inspiring others and motivating them to give their best effort.

1. The "Reset Ritual"

At the start of each day, ask yourself:

- *What kind of leader do I want to be today?*
- *What energy do I want to bring to my interactions?*

Write down three words (e.g., calm, focused, compassionate) and use them as your guiding intentions.

2. "Micro Wins Tracker"

At the end of each day, note three small victories, no matter how minor they seem. This practice rewires your brain to focus on progress rather than setbacks.

3. "Future You" Visualization

Visualize yourself five years from now as the leader you aspire to be. Picture how you handle challenges, inspire others, and maintain balance. Let this vision guide your actions today.

Power Exercise: Mindset Reboot Plan

Goal: Replace limiting beliefs with empowering ones.

- **Identify a Limiting Belief**: Write down one thought that holds you back (e.g., "I'm not good at public speaking.").

- **Reframe It**: Turn it into a growth-oriented belief (e.g., "Every presentation is a chance to improve my speaking skills.").

- **Act on It**: Set one actionable step to challenge this belief (e.g., volunteer to lead the next meeting).

Each of these exercises assists you to consciously focus on developing your mindset and shaping it into one that supports the type of leader you want to be. Identifying what might be holding you back from embracing this mindset is essential to making an integral part of how you lead.

Yet, to maintain the growth mindset, you need to be focused on your own growth, modeling the importance of learning and being open to change for others. My leadership journey has taught me to stick to my values and shape my mindset toward a positive path while keeping my focus on how I can support and motivate others.

While weaknesses will appear, your focus as a leader should always be on maximizing the strengths of those you lead. A growth mindset allows you to see how various team members' strengths complement each other. Being a responsible leader means being open to pushing others to grow themselves, but not to the point where you ignore their challenges. Instead, you work with them to achieve the success for both your family and your business.

Conclusion: The Right Mindset Is the Foundation of Success

The mindset of an unshakable leader transforms challenges into opportunities, setbacks into lessons, and dreams into actionable plans. Cultivate this mindset daily, and you'll inspire others to follow your example of clarity, resilience, and hope.

When you lead with the right mindset, you also inspire others to step up as leaders, showing them how essential their mindset is to their own leadership abilities. Perhaps, however, you have struggled with maintaining a positive mindset. The next chapter is about exploring how you craft a mindset that supports your leadership, regardless of the situation.

Notes

_____

_____

_____

_____

_____

_____

_____

_____

_____

_____

_____

_____

_____

_____

_____

Chapter 10

Cultivating Positive Leadership

"A positive mindset and attitude are contagious."
—Pam Pabla

10

Introduction:
The Essence of Positivity

Positivity is not about denying problems or being overly cheerful; it's about approaching challenges with a constructive and hopeful mindset. Positive leadership transforms teams, families, and communities by creating environments where collaboration, trust, and innovation thrive.

Negativity contributes to a closed mindset, where you approach a situation focused only on the problem, not potential solutions. Moving forward as a leader is more difficult when you have a negative or narrow way of thinking. On the other hand, positivity does not mean you don't see the problem, but that you are open to multiple solutions and opportunities to resolve the issues in a way that benefits those around you.

Perhaps you have dealt with significant challenges, testing your ability to remain positive. Let's discover why positivity in your leadership is essential to your success, as well as ways you can develop positivity and interweave it throughout your role as a leader, no matter the situation.

Why Positivity Is Essential in Leadership

Positivity in leadership fosters a motivating environment. It sets the tone and shapes the culture while encouraging others to adopt similar attitudes by modeling accountability, responsibility, and faithfulness. Research indicates positive leadership behaviors generate positive relational energy, enhancing work performance and morale.

Imagine how this translates to those you lead. Positive leaders encourage open dialogue by showing empathy and compassion, making their team members feel valued and respected. Think about your own life experience. When you feel valued and respected, does it not empower you to engage more, making a greater effort to achieve success? As a leader, your positivity helps others engage and thus gives you more skills and experience to utilize to achieve your business's goals.

Let's return to your family for a moment. What are your family's goals, both as a group and individually? Are there ways to positively engage, fostering an environment that empowers your spouse and children to give their best effort and engage fully with the rest of the family?

Be positive in approaching your family, showing appreciation for their efforts and acknowledging how their contributions benefit others. Positivity helps you to teach your children how to approach challenges, viewing obstacles as opportunities for development, thus encouraging them to be resilient while tackling issues creatively and collaboratively.

No matter how great a leader you are, you cannot achieve success without help from those around you. A proactive approach improves immediate outcomes while cultivating long-term adaptability for those within your family or team.

Here are some practical strategies for developing positivity throughout your life and leadership. First, model the attitude and mindset you want those under your leadership to have. Demonstrate positivity through your actions, showing gratitude and resilience. As you model it, then you inspire others to follow your example.

Secondly, foster open communication. Do not be judgmental or shut down others when they attempt to express themselves. Use open-ended questions to encourage dialogue and feedback, thus building trust and understanding. Doing so helps you to see others not just as part of a team, but as unique individuals who bring their talents and experience to a variety of situations. If they express a desire to learn more or want to track down a specific growth path, then support their efforts to learn through training and mentorship.

My children both had unique interests and talents. Instead of focusing solely on what they struggled with or couldn't do, I listened to them and provided support as they pursued their interests and capitalized on their strengths. It was not always easy to see them make choices that didn't quite align with my vision for them, but ultimately, it was more important to stay the course and celebrate their successes, while helping them to grow through their failures. I was empathetic when things were not going their way, but also helped them to develop strategies to deal with the setbacks.

Leadership is not about providing all the answers but fostering an environment where your family or team feels engaged enough to find the answers for themselves. By showing understanding and empathy during challenging times, you will champion a sense of support and community. As a leader, you must also avoid sinking into toxic positivity, minimizing negative emotions or ignoring them altogether. Effective leaders acknowledge challenges while maintaining a constructive and supportive approach. This balance is key to responsible, accountable, and faithful leadership that embraces positivity.

Toxic positivity in leadership undermines trust, ultimately damaging workplace culture and performance. The issue isn't positivity but excessive optimism that dismisses genuine feelings or the real struggles being faced by those under your leadership.

When leaders prioritize extreme positivity, their team might feel pressured to suppress information that doesn't support the leadership's optimistic viewpoint. This suppression creates an environment of silence, where critical information does not reach leadership, resulting in a disconnect that negatively impacts productivity. Issues grow simply because leaders lack the information to address them properly.

When problems do arise, the lack of constructive conversations hinders effective problem solving and limits the creativity of those you are leading. Urgent concerns get downplayed, leading to missed opportunities for growth and improvement and emotional exhaustion. In high-pressure environments, the pressure to keep up the positivity exacerbates stress and contributes to burnout and a culture of distrust.

As a positive leader, do not focus so heavily on positivity that you dismiss others' concerns. Listen to them without judgment and address their concerns authentically. Talk about both successes and challenges, allowing your team to express concerns—model vulnerability for those you lead. Admitting you don't have all the answers demonstrates that talking about your concerns and asking for help is okay. The pathway to resilience lies not in maintaining artificial positivity but in creating an environment where challenges are embraced and exploring failures means learning opportunities.

Positivity is essential to effective leadership. It nurtures a supportive culture, enhances everyone's problem solving and creativity, and inspires others to collaborate, engage, and perform best. Leaders and their teams thrive under positive, balanced leadership, navigating challenges with optimism and resilience.

Core Practices of Positive Leadership

1. **Uplifting Communication**

   - Replace criticism with constructive feedback. Instead of, "You're behind schedule," say, "What resources do you need to meet your goal?"

2. **Celebrate Effort, Not Just Results**

   - Recognize the process, not just the outcome. Celebrate perseverance, creativity, and growth.

3. **Practice "Gratitude in Action"**

   - Show gratitude through small but meaningful gestures, such as handwritten notes, verbal praise, or acts of service.

Power Exercise: Positivity Reset

Goal: Shift a negative environment into a positive one.

- **Identify Negative Patterns**: Note recurring complaints or conflicts in your group.

- **Reframe Conversations**: Introduce solution-focused dialogue by asking, "What's one step we can take to move forward?"

- **Celebrate Small Wins**: Acknowledge progress and contributions publicly to build momentum.

Conclusion: The Power of Positivity

Positivity is the energy that fuels progress and connection. A positive attitude inspires and uplifts others by transforming challenges into opportunities. Incorporating hope, encouragement, resilience, and confidence into situations creates a ripple effect of empowerment in every sphere you lead.

Working to maintain a positive mindset impacts your leadership by supporting a mindset focused on growth and creativity. Additionally, a positive mindset shifts your thinking, drawing the type of solutions and circumstances that support your success and help others to thrive.

Notes

_____

_____

_____

_____

_____

_____

_____

_____

_____

_____

_____

_____

_____

_____

_____

_____

Chapter 11

The Power of Thoughts

"You attract what you think and feel."
—Pam Pabla

11

Introduction: Thoughts as the Foundation of Leadership

Your thoughts shape your world. They influence how you interpret challenges, communicate with others, and envision success. By intentionally guiding your internal dialogue, you can transform your leadership and your impact on those around you.

How do your thoughts shape your leadership? Take a moment to reflect on your daily thoughts. We just discussed the importance of positivity in leadership, including how critical it is to foster a creative, growth-oriented culture. Do you find yourself slipping into negative thoughts, focused on what is going wrong and spiraling into scenarios where everything goes wrong?

Understand that leaders' thoughts dictate whether they approach challenges confidently and creatively or hesitate, bogged down by failures. When you are focused on what went wrong, it becomes a filter that impacts your decisions as a leader. A leader's thoughts directly influence their decision-making processes. Positive thinking enhances creativity and innovation, allowing you to see the possibilities and opportunities wrapped up in the challenges you face.

Thoughts are also interlinked with your emotions—understanding this relationship contributes to the development of your emotional intelligence (EQ). When you have a high EQ, you regulate your emotions, essential for maintaining composure and making rational decisions under pressure. Fostering a mindset grounded in empathy and understanding allows you to connect with others, boosting morale and engagement.

Your inner dialogue shapes how you interact with others. Positive, constructive thoughts create an inspiring presence, while negative ones dampen collaboration. Additionally, your thoughts should align with values and faith, strengthening clarity and conviction in your leadership. Engaging in self-reflection to identify and understand your thought patterns and determine whether they are in alignment with your values is one of the first steps in shifting them from a negative outlook to a more positive one.

Thoughts are fundamental to effective leadership, shaping how leaders perceive their roles, interact with their teams, and navigate challenges. By cultivating positive thinking, emotional intelligence, and an environment of trust, faithful leaders lay a strong foundation for dynamic and successful leadership. Through ongoing self-reflection, active listening, and a commitment to learning, leaders can improve their effectiveness and inspire and elevate those around them.

Core Values of Faithful Leaders

Your core values and beliefs shape your thoughts. When you have a clear understanding of your values, your thoughts align with them, thus giving you a solid foundation to be successful. However, when your thoughts are not aligned with your values, then your thoughts do not contribute to successful leadership but limit your ability to lead with confidence and empathy.

Effective leaders embody core values, such as integrity, empathy, respect, and adaptability, shaping their decision making, inspiring others toward success. As we explore each of these values, you begin to see how they all contribute to your accountability, responsibility, and faithfulness.

- **Integrity** – Leaders who value integrity are honest, ethical, and consistent, gaining respect from others.

- **Empathy** – Leaders understand the perspectives and feelings of others, enabling leaders to build strong relationships and foster a collaborative environment.

- **Respect** – Respecting others' contributions and viewpoints creates a positive environment where everyone feels valued, whether at home or work.

- **Adaptability** – Leaders embrace change and demonstrate flexibility, allowing them to guide others through uncertainty and maintain morale during transitions.

- **Passion** – Genuine passion motivates leaders, impacting the energy and enthusiasm of those they lead, serving as a real inspiration.

- **Resilience** – Leaders recover from setbacks and model resilience for others, helping to instill the same resilience in those who are also facing challenging situations.

My whole focus as a leader is the type of person I want to be, what I want to model for others, and the mindset I want to use to shape my perspective. I focus on my thoughts, making conscious decisions regarding how I want to think, the values I want to align with, and my choices.

Clearly, the core values you embrace shape your thoughts, behaviors, and decision-making processes, and influence the culture and environment you create for those around you. Embodying your values authentically is the best way to instill confidence in others and develop mutual respect and shared success.

Effective leadership is rooted in a commitment to core values that guide actions and inspire those around them. Leaders who take the time to articulate and model their values cultivate a committed and engaged workforce, driving their organizations and families toward success.

Daily Thought Practices for Leaders

1. The "5-Minute Mental Reset"

When overwhelmed, take five minutes to write down:

- One worry or negative thought.
- One positive belief to replace it.
- One small action to reinforce the new thought.

2. Thought Anchors

Create a list of empowering affirmations or quotes. Repeat them during moments of doubt to re-center your mindset.

Power Exercise: The "Thought Garden"

Goal: Cultivate empowering thoughts and remove mental weeds.

- **Visualize**: Picture your mind as a garden. Each positive thought is a flower, and each negative thought is a weed.

- **Plant Seeds**: Identify one empowering belief you want to nurture.

- **Pull Weeds**: Identify one limiting belief and replace it with an empowering affirmation.

Final Reflection: The Leadership Blueprint

Goal: Integrate all nine chapters into a cohesive leadership practice.

1. **Define Your Pillars**: Write your personal definitions of accountability, responsibility, and faithfulness.

2. **Create a Weekly Ritual**: Dedicate time to reflect on your mindset, celebrate progress, and refine your leadership approach.

3. **Practice the Daily Essentials**:

   - Mindset Check-In: What am I focusing on today?

   - Positivity Moment: How can I inspire hope in someone today?

   - Thought Audit: What belief is shaping my decisions right now?

Conclusion: Thoughts Shape Reality

Your thoughts are the seeds of your leadership legacy. Leadership is not about being perfect in life; it is about being purposeful, present, and faithful to your mission.

As you step into the next chapter of your leadership journey, remember that every thought, action, and interaction can inspire and empower change. Lead with clarity, positivity, and faithfulness, and you'll leave an unshakable legacy that endures.

Notes

_____

_____

_____

_____

_____

_____

_____

_____

_____

_____

_____

_____

_____

_____

_____

_____

Part Five

Conclusion

A Legacy of Leadership

"Your story is the greatest and most empowering legacy."
—Pam Pabla

Leadership is the art of leaving a meaningful mark on the lives and environments you influence. It is not confined to professional titles or hierarchical positions but lies in the intention, actions, and care you bring to every relationship and responsibility.

This book has guided you through the principles that build unshakeable leadership, a framework that enables you to lead with strength, authenticity, and purpose.

As we revisit the six pillars of unshakable leadership, remember that each chapter was designed to help you navigate life's challenges while positively shaping the world around you.

Revisiting the pillars and the preceding chapters, you have explored a comprehensive framework for unshakable leadership:

1. **Accountability** – Owning your decisions and outcomes.

2. **Responsibility** – Serving others with integrity and compassion.

3. **Faith** – Trusting in a higher purpose or plan, particularly in times of uncertainty.

4. **Mindset** – Maintaining a growth-oriented and resilient mental posture.

5. **Positivity** – Infusing hope, warmth, and solution-focused thinking into every interaction.

6. **The Power of Thoughts** – Recognizing how inner dialogue shapes actions and results.

Whether leading in a corporate environment, guiding a nonprofit, nurturing a family, or building a community initiative, these pillars act as cornerstones that steady your leadership foundation. Through stories, real-life examples, and spiritual undertones, each chapter has unveiled how accountability, responsibility, faith, mindset, positivity, and intentional thought patterns weave together to create leadership that life's storms cannot shake.

Creating a Lasting Impact

Leading does not require you to be given a formal title or position. You demonstrate leadership by how you choose to respond to challenges, how you treat others, and how you uphold your values. As you reflect on your immediate sphere of influence, be it family, colleagues, or friends, identify one small, consistent act that can uplift or transform your environment (likely, weekly check-ins with others or developing a daily gratitude practice).

Each pillar requires consistent attention to remain vibrant. Regularly revisiting these chapters and activities can assist you in maintaining these foundational pillars of your leadership. Be honest with yourself on your progress, and don't be afraid to admit areas where you still might need more conscious effort.

To hold yourself accountable, schedule quarterly (or monthly) mini-retreats to gauge your progress and how well you embody accountability, responsibility, and faith. Use these moments to reset goals and reaffirm your commitment to lead with these core values.

Expand Your Circle of Influence

As your leadership grows sturdier, you become a beacon for others seeking purpose-driven models. Mentoring, volunteering, or simply listening attentively to someone else's struggles can multiply the impact of what you've learned.

Challenge: Invite at least one colleague or friend to read this book or discuss the pillars with you. Share insights, address stumbling blocks, and celebrate victories together.

Sustaining Your Pillars in Everyday Life

Accountability:

Keep owning your outcomes—be it success or setbacks. This honesty cultivates deeper self-respect and trust among those you lead.

Responsibility:

Approach each interaction with the question, "How can I serve or support this person?" Small acts of kindness ripple outward powerfully.

Faith:

In uncertain seasons, remember that faith does not promise ease; it promises purpose. Even unanswered questions or delayed outcomes can refine your character and mission.

Mindset:

Nurture a growth-oriented attitude. Practice reframing tough situations into opportunities for learning. Reflect on each obstacle with curiosity instead of dread.

Positivity:

Maintain an environment where optimism feels authentic and solution-focused. Validate real problems but spotlight progress and potential wherever possible.

The Power of Thoughts:

Keep your inner dialogue supportive, compassionate, and forward-looking. By directing your thoughts wisely, you steer not just your mind but also your actions and outcomes.

Continuing Your Growth

1. **Seek Inspiration and Knowledge**

   - Leadership is a lifelong journey. Supplement your experiences with books, podcasts, seminars, or spiritual gatherings that broaden your perspective and keep your motivation renewed.

2. **Engage a Support Network**

   - Surround yourself with mentors, peers, or communities who reflect the same commitment to accountability, responsibility, faith, mindset, positivity, and intentional thinking. Collaborative growth keeps complacency at bay.

3. Reflect on Your Unique Purpose

- Revisit your talents, past experiences, and heartfelt convictions. Where do they naturally intersect with the needs of your family, workplace, or community? This sweet spot is often the gateway to your most fulfilling leadership contributions.

A Final Encouragement

Unshakable leadership is not about personal glory—it is about effecting lasting change in hearts, minds, and systems around you. By living each pillar—embodying accountability in decision making, acting responsibly to serve others, maintaining faith amid unpredictability, harnessing a resilient mindset, cultivating genuine positivity, and guiding your thoughts productively—you become a transformative force in every realm you touch.

You've seen how a mother's resolve can shape a child's brighter future, how intentional leadership kindles hope within others, and how faith sparks creativity in a crisis. Now, it's your turn to carry these lessons forward. Keep refining each principle, be patient with your growth, and trust that even small, faithful steps create profound ripples over time.

Thank you for journeying through these chapters. May your leadership radiate unshakable strength, grounded in accountability, responsibility, and faith, and be enriched by a constructive mindset, positive perspective, and carefully chosen thoughts. In doing so, you stand poised to leave a legacy that uplifts, unites, and inspires generations to come.

Leadership is not about perfection—it's about progress, persistence, and purpose. Living the six pillars of accountability, responsibility, faithfulness, mindset, positivity, and the power of thoughts creates a leadership legacy that uplifts, empowers, and transforms.

You've seen how a mother's determination can shape a child's future, how faith can guide a team through uncertainty, and how intentional thoughts can spark meaningful change. Now it's your turn to lead with clarity and conviction.

Remember this: Small, consistent actions compound into profound results. Each moment you choose accountability, serve responsibly, trust in faithfulness, nurture a growth mindset, exude positivity, or steer your thoughts with purpose, you're building a legacy that impacts generations.

The world needs unshakable leaders like you. Thank you for embarking on this journey. May your leadership radiate strength, compassion, and inspiration, leaving an indelible mark on everyone you touch.

Notes

Acknowledgments

Gratitude is the foundation of every meaningful journey, and as I reflect on the path that led to *Unshakable Leadership,* my heart is overflowing.

This book is not just the product of my experiences but also the result of the people God placed in my life, each one bringing wisdom, encouragement, and divine timing.

I am genuinely thankful for every soul who walked with me, believed in me, challenged me, and lifted me in prayer and presence.

Thank You, God, for all You have done and continue to do in my life. Thank You for trusting me with this assignment and blessing me with abundant love and support.

I am humbled by the people You have surrounded me with—family and friends whose encouragement, strength, and faith have carried me through this journey. Their belief in me on the days when the words would not come or the vision felt too complicated to be true has enlightened my path to overcome challenges, rise above doubt, and keep writing with purpose, passion, and unwavering faith.

I thank everyone who supported me during my growth, challenges, and personal discovery. Your kindness, love, and support became a steppingstone in the chapters of this book. Your presence always mattered whether you were there for a moment or a milestone.

This book is not written by one voice alone—it carries the echo of many hearts, woven together to complete what felt like a dream and bring it into reality.

Creator

To my Heavenly Father: You are the Author and Finisher of my faith. This journey would not exist without You. Your truth, grace, and unwavering love have inspired every word I have written.

Family, Friends, Colleagues & Mentors

To my mother, Surinder: I am truly blessed to have you. Your quiet strength, unwavering faith, and boundless love have shaped the foundation of my life, my values, and the woman I am today.

To my beloved father, Harmohinder: Though you are not here physically, your love lives on in me. I honor your name and your legacy through every word in this book.

To my husband, Parm: Your love, patience, and quiet strength have been my foundation. You've stood by me in every season with unwavering belief.

To my daughters, Rupam and Rhea: You are my heart. Rupam, your brilliance and grace remind me daily of strength in love. Rhea, your joyful spirit teaches me to see beauty in every moment.

To my son, Taygveer: You are a true son. Your love and honor bring peace to our home, and how you care for Rupam brings me joy and pride.

To Sahib, our sweet miracle: You are already a light in our hearts. Your life is a promise, a blessing, and a legacy in motion.

To Charlie, our beloved companion: You are our family. Your love, loyalty, and presence brought peace through every writing day. You reminded me to rest, breathe, and be me.

To Harbhajan Singh Ubhi and Paramjit Kaur Ubhi: You are like parents to me. Your humility, wisdom, and loving hearts have left a lasting impact on our entire family. I will never forget the day you told me to "plant a seed"—that seed became this book. Your lives have inspired generations, and I am blessed beyond words to walk in the warmth of your example.

To Gurpreet and Kuljeet Ubhi: Thank you for raising a wonderful son and for embracing our family with such grace and warmth. I am so blessed to walk this journey of family with you.

Nickveer and Atarveer Ubhi, you are more than family—you're like sons to me. I am proud of the incredible men you are.

To my brother and his family—Jas Saini—thank you for always protecting and believing in me. I am proud to be your sister, and I cherish our bond.

My beloved cousin brothers—Pawan Budwal, Jag Singh Budwal, JP Budwal, Sunny Saini, Michael Saini, and Paul Saini—I am truly grateful for each of you and our bond.

To Nav, Donny Sandher, and family: Nav, you are my soul sister and dearest friend. You have held my hand, lifted my head, and loved me through every season of life. Thank you for being my strength and my heart's safe place.

To Swarna Shivdasani, Sameer Gidwani, and family: Swarna, my soul sister and my daughters' angel, your heart is pure, your friendship unwavering. You are a divine gift. Thank you for your love, strength, and constant presence in our lives.

To Moleshree, Suchit Khanna, and family: Molly, thank you for being a sister in truth, strength, and love. Your presence is a blessing in my life. Rajveer and Viraaj bring such joy and light with their laughter and playful hearts. Manvi Juneja is a gem whose warmth and grace shine so beautifully. May your home always be filled with love, health, and divine favor.

To Sarah Gopie: You've been a part of our lives for so many years, and to me, you are more than family—you are like a daughter. Your love, kindness, and unwavering support toward my family mean the world, and I treasure you deeply.

To Rachelle Purewal: Rachelle, you are more than my daughter's best friend—you're family. Your strength, loyalty, and quiet wisdom shine so brightly. I admire the beautiful heart you lead with, and I am so grateful to have you in our lives.

To Renita Lobo, my daughter's dance teacher and a true angel: Your guidance gave her wings and a beautiful way to express her soul. Your friendship, kindness, and unwavering support have meant more than words can say.

To all my cousins, brothers and sisters, and cherished family members: Whether your name is mentioned or not, please know that you hold a special place in my heart. Your love, prayers, and presence in my life mean more to me than words can express. I am deeply grateful for each one of you.

Rosy Saini, Navi Saini, Raman, Ruby Saini, Rajni Dhamrait, JP, Pawan, Jag, Sandy, Pawanjot, Navi Lal, Ruby Rangi, Kiran, Punam, Raju, Pinky, Rosy, Neetu, Dave, Karam, Jas Marwaha, Simran, nickiSanjeet Saini, Sunny, Michael and Paul, Dil Banga, Jas Banga, and Ritu—your kind heart and radiant positivity have been a blessing. Thank you for your love.

To all my uncles and aunts: Your love, wisdom, and blessings have helped shape the person I am today. While I may not have mentioned each of you by name, please know that I appreciate and cherish you all deeply.

Kuldip and Pushpa Budwal, your love is like that of parents. You have covered me with protection, care, and prayers. I am truly grateful and blessed for you both!

Hargurdip and Kulbir Saini, your presence has been a gift of strength and support.

Mohinder and Gurbax Saini, thank you for your encouragement and love! Uncle Gurbax, I am proud to see you officially acclaimed as the Liberal candidate for Fleetwood–Port Kells in the 2025 general election.

Gurcharan and Amarjit Budwal, thank you for always showing love and guidance.

To Aunt Gurdev Budwal: Your presence has been a gift of love!

To Manjit and Surjit Rangi: Thank you for your quiet love, heartfelt blessings, and thoughtful presence in my life. I'm truly grateful for you both.

Manmohan and Raghvir Saini, I am grateful for your warmth.

Nephews and Nieces

To all my beloved nieces and nephews: Each of you brings so much joy, light, and meaning into my life. Watching you grow into kind, thoughtful, and inspiring individuals fills my heart with pride. You are deeply loved, and I carry you in my prayers always.

To Jyoti Gill: Thank you for your heartfelt support, patience, and quiet strength throughout this journey. Your presence has been a true blessing to me and my family, and I am deeply grateful for your care and kindness.

My Spiritual Family

To my spiritual father, Pastor Prem Masih-Gill: Thank you for recognizing God's calling on my life and speaking it into existence. Your prophetic words became the spark that led to this book. Your prayers, wisdom, and spiritual covering have been a guiding light through every step of this journey. I also lift up your beloved wife, Aunty Ji, in prayer—may God's healing, strength, and peace be with her always.

I also want to extend my warmest acknowledgment to your beautiful family, who I've come to know through your words and stories. Though we haven't met in person, their presence has touched my heart deeply: Elaine and Damien Masih-Jones, Lisa Masih-Gill, Claire and Nicholas Masih-Gill, and your precious grandson, Louie Prince. May God continue to bless and guide each one of them.

To Pastor Olufemi Adegun: Thank you for your spiritual counsel and encouragement. Your prayers uplifted me during critical moments and reminded me of God's unwavering faithfulness. I also acknowledge your wife and family with respect and gratitude. May God continue to bless and guide you in all you do.

To Pastor Vishal and Pastor Rafiqua Rangha: Your unwavering commitment to truth, purpose, and God's calling inspires me daily. Pastor Vishal, you are a true spiritual brother whose faith and leadership have left a lasting imprint on my journey. Pastor Rafiqua, your wisdom, grace, and kindness are gifts I carry with me—thank you for being a beacon of strength and compassion. I also lovingly acknowledge Daddy Ji, whose presence brings a deep sense of love, legacy, and quiet strength to your beautiful family.

Summer Rangha, you are like a daughter to me. Your joyful spirit, pure heart, and deep love for God are rare and beautiful. To your loving husband Eric, and to your dear siblings Désirée and Elijah— may God's blessings always surround you. And sweet Diesel, your loyal companion, who brings light and laughter wherever he goes.

To Pastor Subash Gill: Your anointed worship blesses many. Your songs usher in presence, peace, and power. Thank you for inspiring not only my spirit but the spirit of my entire family. Your love and light have truly made a difference.

To Brother Vikas, Beena Rangha, and their daughters Tabitha and Annabella: Thank you for being a steady support system in prayer and faith.

To Brother Younas Masih and Vimi Masih: Thank you for your faithful prayers and spiritual support for our families. You both are truly a blessings in our lives.

To all my church and spiritual family and friends: Your support, faith, and love have been a source of strength. You have helped carry me through this journey's most important and sacred moments.

Family Friends

To Ravi and Pooja Bedi and family: Your constant support, kindness, and friendship have meant so much to our family. Krish, Natasha, and Ankit bring such joy and warmth. We are truly grateful to have you in our lives.

To Harminder Saini and Tejinder Saini: You have been a loving part of our extended family. I appreciate your constant support and generosity.

To the Dhir family – Renu Aunty and Ramesh Uncle, Sanjay and Kanika, and your wonderful children—thank you for the kindness, warmth, and grace you bring into our lives. Your genuine care, support, and positive presence have touched our hearts. We are truly grateful to have you in our lives.

Div Saini, you are like a son to me. Your presence, kindness, and support have been a true blessing.

To Geetu Arora, Jazzy Arora, and their families: Thank you for being a part of our lives and for being such great friends! We are blessed to have you in our lives.

To Bill and Davinder Aulukh, and your families: Thank you for your friendship, encouragement, and support. You have been a beautiful part of my journey.

To Dave and Tejinder Walia, and your families: Your kindness and encouragement have meant so much to me. We are grateful for your presence in our lives.

To Narinder and Neelu Talwar and family: Thank you for all the support, love, and kindness.

To Anita and Jeevan Punni: Thank you for your enduring friendship and support. You have been cherished family friends for many years, and your presence in our lives is truly appreciated.

To Bobby More and family: Bobby, it has been a joy watching you grow into the incredible lawyer and person you are today. I am proud to have known you since you were a child.

To Harman Heir: Your support, professionalism, and kindness have been truly appreciated. Thank you for being part of this journey.

To Raman Sahota: Thank you for your constant encouragement and support. Your positivity and belief in me have meant so much along this journey.

To Gugan Mander, Sony Mander, Daljit Purewal, Daljit Jutla, and Gurinder Pawan: Thank you for your friendship and support.

To Shirly Lobo, who lovingly takes care of my dog Charlie when we go on vacation: Thank you. Your love and care for animals is beautiful and admirable.

To Devinder, Manjit (Mini), and their families: Your warmth and friendship have turned neighbors into lifelong companions. Thank you for always being there.

To Kuljeet, Nav Chhinzer, and family: Thank you for being more like family than friends and for giving us so much love.

To our past therapists—Lauren Backman, Nicky Praseuth, and Ashley Cohen—thank you for your dedication and compassion and for the support you gave to my daughter and our family. Your work changes lives.

To Inderjit and Pukhraj: Your kindness and love toward my daughters have meant so much. Thank you for being part of our lives.

To Paige from Skin with Paige: Thank you for your professionalism, positivity, and the light you bring to your work. Your kindness and inspiration are truly appreciated.

To Inderjit and Taranjit Guraya: Thank you for your friendship, kindness, and continued support over the years. Your presence in our lives is truly appreciated.

To Mahind Raj and Kiran Kanwar: Thank you for your warm friendship and continued support. Your kindness and presence have been a true blessing to our family.

My Team and Partners

To my team at Pam Pabla Insurance and Financial Services Inc.: Thank you for walking this journey with me and for the heart you bring to our work each day. Your dedication, care, and commitment to our clients have helped shape the foundation of our success.

I would also like to extend my heartfelt gratitude to the incredible individuals who were part of this journey in the past. Your contributions have been meaningful and appreciated: Cris Jose, Manali Naik, Bikram Singh, Anuradha Sondhi, Payal Anand, Sukhjot (Bob) Kamboj, my brother Jas Saini, and Summer Rangha. Thank you for the role you played in helping us grow and serve with excellence.

To Clint Gomez, a valued team member for the past five years: Your excellence, loyalty, and unwavering faith have not gone unnoticed. Your humility, respect, and how you treat my business speak volumes about your character. I'm deeply grateful for your dedication and the heart you bring to everything you do.

To Manvi Juneja, thank you for joining the team with such energy, professionalism, and a fresh perspective. Your attention to detail, positive spirit, and commitment to excellence have already brought so much value. I am truly grateful and look forward to the continued growth and success we will achieve together as a team.

To Rosy Saini: Thank you for being family and a constant source of encouragement. Your kindness, positivity, and fresh perspective continue to bring light and meaning to my work. I'm truly grateful for your unwavering support.

Community & Collaboration

A special thank you to Rina Gill of Hype Advertising Agency: Your creativity, marketing expertise, and dedication played a key role in bringing visibility and energy to this project. I'm grateful for your partnership and the many ways you've helped elevate my message and brand with excellence.

Thank you, Christine Hull, Social Media Trainer, Community Leader, and Founder of MAWB (Moms at Work in Business)—a dynamic networking group for businesswomen in Mississauga and the surrounding area—and 100 Women Who Care Mississauga. Your vision, leadership, and passion for empowering women through meaningful connections and education are truly inspiring. I'm honored to be a part of both communities as a sponsor and even more grateful to call you a friend.

A special thank you to my brother, Jag Singh Budwal, owner and CEO of Dream Productions, for capturing the essence of this journey through his lens. His eye for detail, and passion for visual storytelling, brought this project to life beautifully and meaningfully. I'm grateful for his talent, time, and the love he poured into this photoshoot.

A heartfelt thank you to Hark S. Aulakh for capturing beautiful moments through his lens in the past. His creativity and professionalism have left a lasting impression, and I'm grateful for his support on my journey.

To Monet Studios and the talented Judy Chan: Thank you for the beautiful space and experience during my book photoshoot. Judy, your kindness, creativity, and professionalism made the entire process so enjoyable and memorable. I'm truly grateful for your warmth and the care you put into your work.

Thank you, Amandeep Kaloti, at Mirrorless Productions, for your creative support and contributions behind the scenes. Your work added an extra touch of excellence to this journey.

My heartfelt thanks, Sarbie Gill, at Makeup by Sarbie, for your artistry and skill. Your beautiful makeup enhanced the entire look and feel of this project with elegance and professionalism.

Thank you, Rav, at Enara Beauty, for your expert styling and thoughtful touch—your work added confidence and polish to every moment of this journey.

Leadership - Desjardins

Thank you to Mr. Guy Cormier, President and CEO of Desjardins Group. Your leadership, vision, and unwavering commitment to people-first values have deeply inspired me. I am proud to be part of an organization with integrity, innovation, and care for community and culture. Thank you for continuing to lead with purpose and impact.

Thank you, Valérie Lavoie, for your exceptional leadership and steadfast commitment to supporting agents and clients. Your grace, wisdom, and dedication to excellence have inspired me on my journey. I am truly grateful for the empowering culture you help create within Desjardins—one where people and purpose come first.

Thank you, Benaaz Aronis, for your unwavering support, encouragement, and leadership at Desjardins. Your positivity, approachability, and commitment to helping others grow have made a meaningful impact on my journey. I'm genuinely grateful for your guidance and the inspiration you bring to our network.

Thank you, Raymond Bentivegna, for your steady leadership and continued support. Your guidance, professionalism, and belief in your agents' success have created a strong foundation for growth in our region. I appreciate your encouragement and trust as we serve our communities purposefully and carefully.

Thank you, Rehan Bhanji, National Best Practice Leader at Desjardins Insurance, for your exceptional leadership and commitment to raising the standard of excellence across our network. Your insights, guidance, and dedication to best practices have been truly impactful. I appreciate your efforts in supporting agents and fostering a culture of continuous growth and improvement.

To the Corporate and Desjardins Family, colleagues, mentors, professional partners, fellow leaders and friends:

Thank you for your support, guidance, and friendship along the way. Your belief in me, and your encouragement through the many seasons of my business journey, has made a meaningful and lasting impact. I am genuinely grateful for your shared wisdom, collaboration, and leadership.

Howie Burrows, Dina El-Zeinab, Linda Pasutto, Micah Neale, Dawit Hamilton, Kenneth Lindhardsen, Brad Banville, David Owens, Neeta Sharma, Harry Movois, Kim Robinson, Darren Rodrigues, Sandra Jurkovic, Gur Sohi, Harpreet Pawar, Harpreet Formay, Hardeep Ghuman, Bikram Singh, Sukhjot (Bob) Kamboj, Baljinder (Billie) Dhuga, Vince Ippolito, Jason Sant, Kevin D'Souza, Dina Constantinou, Patricia Velasco, Mike Tullo, Nando Tullo, Rachel May Poy, Shawn Bishundat, Todd O'Donnell, Amit and Harpreet Bhagirath, Renu Dhir, Ravinder Singh, Maninder Chhibber, and Sujata Chauhan:

You have each played a meaningful role in shaping my journey, and I am truly grateful.

Thank you, Darryl Coutinho, for being kind and supportive.

Academic & Professional Mentorship

Thank you, John A.F. McNeil, Associate Dean, Continuous Professional Learning at Humber College's Longo Faculty of Business, for our thoughtful connection a few years ago. In 2018, I had the pleasure of hiring a student from your program, and I appreciated your kind acknowledgment of that collaboration. It's always a privilege to support emerging professionals, and I'm grateful for the bridge between education and industry that your leadership represents.

Thank you, Annette Palalas, Professor at Mohawk College – School of Business, for the wonderful memories and collaboration we shared years ago. Your dedication to teaching, and kind, thoughtful nature, have always stood out to me. It's been a privilege to know you, not only as a respected educator but also as a friend. I admire your passion for empowering students and making a meaningful impact through education.

Thank you to the Insurance Career Connections team for your dedication to promoting careers in the insurance industry and supporting professionals at every stage of their journey. Your efforts to bridge talent with opportunity are genuinely inspiring. I'm grateful for your work and your positive impact in shaping a stronger, more connected industry.

Thank you, Tanya Anaya, Educator Coordinator for the CIP Program, for your dedication to advancing professional development within the insurance industry. Your support and coordination have been instrumental in helping educators and students thrive. I genuinely appreciate the opportunity to work alongside you, and admire your commitment to the CIP community.

Thank you, Deborah Diflorio, Training Facilitator at Desjardins, for your ongoing support and friendship. Your passion for training, warm heart, and uplifting spirit have always made a difference. I feel especially blessed that we share a birthday—a reminder of the joy and connection we've shared through our professional paths and personal bonds.

Teachers and Principals

To all the teachers and principals who have guided, supported, and nurtured the growth of my family: Thank you. Your dedication to education, your patience, and your ability to inspire are powerful gifts that shape generations. I am deeply grateful for the impact you've had in our lives.

A special shout-out to Norma Dwyer, Principal at Ellwood Memorial Public School and formerly at Lorenville Public School, where she supported my daughter with incredible kindness and care. Your encouragement and leadership have left a lasting imprint on our hearts.

A heartfelt thank you to Ajinder Sehgal (Mrs. A) for the unwavering support, kindness, and encouragement you've shown my daughter. Your understanding and dedication have made a lasting impact on her journey, and I am truly grateful for the difference you have made in her life.

My Clients

To all my valued clients, thank you for your trust in me and my team.

Your belief in our guidance, your loyalty, and the opportunity to walk alongside you in protecting what matters most are privileges I never take for granted. Your stories, goals, and commitment have inspired what is written on these pages.

Because of you, I continue to grow in purpose, leadership, and service. I am truly grateful for the chance to serve you, and I honor your confidence in allowing me to be a part of your life's journey.

Youth Inspiration

A special thank you to Aaron and Neville Gidwani, Anjali and Nitin Sharma, Amaya, Jora Sandher, Samina Chhinzer, Deren and Dana Luis, and Nicky Saini: Your kindness, warmth, and friendship toward Rhea have touched our hearts. Your compassion and joyful presence are a true reflection of what it means to be thoughtful, uplifting, and inspiring young leaders.

TV Shows and Mentors Who Have Driven Me

To Raymond Aaron, thank you for seeing the potential in me, selecting me as a co-author, and guiding me throughout this book journey. You provided the space and direction I needed to complete my manuscript, and your belief in me helped birth this vision into reality.

To Liz, Mikee Patel, Tracy, Patricia, Aysha, Chinmai, Mansi, Waqas, and the entire Raymond Aaron team: Thank you for your support and encouragement throughout this writing adventure. Your guidance has been uplifting and meaningful every step of the way.

To Les Brown: Meeting you virtually on Zoom was a moment I will never forget. Your legendary voice, wisdom, and contagious passion have inspired me deeply.

I'm also grateful to the many motivational leaders and visionaries whose teachings and energy have been part of my journey:

Tony Robbins, Dean Graziosi, Brian Tracy, Jack Canfield, Russell Brunson, Jenna Kutcher, Brendon Burchard, Jamie Kern Lima, Francis Ablola, and Brian Hanson. Through your books, talks, or courses, each of you has helped sharpen my mindset, deepen my mission, and ignite a fire that continues to burn strong.

I'd also like to acknowledge other powerful voices who have left a mark on my growth:

Mel Robbins, Marie Forleo, Robin Sharma, Oprah Winfrey, Ed Mylett, Lisa Nichols, Jay Shetty, Gabby Bernstein, Eric Thomas, Lewis Howes, and Jim Kwik.

Oprah Winfrey, as an American host and television producer, your legacy of compassion, leadership, and storytelling has shaped my understanding of purpose and public voice.

In addition, special thanks to the media outlets and programs that continue to inspire Canadians and amplify meaningful conversations:

CP24, CBC, and Breakfast Television—thank you for sharing stories that matter and consistently highlighting voices from all walks of life.

Health & Wellness Coaches/Entrepreneurship & Empowerment

Taking care of my mind and body has been vital to leading with strength, balance, and peace. I am so grateful to the incredible individuals who have supported my physical wellness and spiritual alignment throughout this journey.

To my Strength Training family at TFW Sauga, thank you for building my physical resilience and confidence.

Cory Fernandes and Susie Ung (Owners), your passion for transformation and heart-led leadership shines through every workout and encounter.

Carmella Sok, Lead Head Coach, thank you for challenging me with strength and fire.

Melizza Mendoza, Student Success Manager, thank you for your joyful encouragement and thoughtful check-ins.

Soubhi Soufan, thank you for your steady support and motivation on the floor.

To my daughter's yoga coach and my best friend, Swarna Shivdasani, at Yoga with Swarna, you are a light. Your guidance on the mat and in life brings me peace, joy, and grounding.

To my dear friend and fitness coach, Renita Lobo, at Super U Fitness, you are an empowering coach and a friend who truly walks beside me. Your workouts energize me, and your belief in women's wellness is inspiring.

To Sarbjeet Kalia at Indian Yoga, thank you for guiding me through my yoga teacher training. Your wisdom and clarity led me to deeper awareness and alignment.

Thank you, Amanda Jeppesen, founder and CEO of Souslaface, for your inspiring leadership and dedication to empowering others through beauty, wellness, and authenticity. Your passion, creativity, and entrepreneurial spirit shine through everything you do.

A special thank you also to your incredible team—Alexandra Fox and Catherine Cramer—for the warmth, professionalism, and care you bring to the experience.

A special shout-out to PinkRockFitness: Your empowering presence on social media is both motivating and refreshing. Your commitment to fitness, positivity, and community shines through your content, and I genuinely appreciate the inspiration you bring to so many of us.

Trusted Healthcare Professionals

To Dr. Rizwan Ahmed Shaikh, MD, thank you for your thoughtful care, kindness, and time spent supporting our family's health. Your professionalism and wisdom are greatly appreciated.

To Dr. Gunjan Maggo, MD, thank you for your warm approach, attentive care, and always taking the time to listen and guide. Your compassion shines through every visit.

To Dr. Neil Gajjar, Associates and Specialists (dentistry), thank you and your incredible team for your professionalism and gentle care. Your clinic has always made our family feel comfortable, well cared for, and informed.

To Dr. Harshvir Aujla, dentist, thank you for your excellent care and genuine warmth. You and your family have not only supported our wellness journey but have also become dear family friends. We are grateful for your kindness and expertise.

To Dr. Sonya Doherty, N.D., a naturopathic doctor at Natural Care Clinic, thank you for your holistic insight and for walking with our family through personalized, meaningful care. Your integrative approach has made a lasting impact.

To Dr. Louse Basic, homeopath at Vibra Med Holistic Core Inc., thank you for your healing touch and deep understanding of homeopathy. Your support in our wellness journey has brought so much balance and clarity.

To Gurpreet (Gary) Jutla, our pharmacist and friend, thank you for your exceptional service and genuine care as both a healthcare provider and a neighbor. Your friendly support and professionalism have meant so much to our family.

To Jazz, Deepi, Jay, and Nav Virdi from Optical Zone, thank you for your excellent service and commitment to quality eye care. Your professionalism and dedication are truly appreciated.

To Lisa Israel, founder and CEO of ABI, registered nurse, psychotherapist, and board-certified behavior analyst, thank you for being part of our family and my daughter's life for so many years. Your care and support mean the world to us.

Inspiration & Community Leaders

A heartfelt thank you to Nav Bhatia, the Superfan, for their inspiring presence and unwavering support: Your story and spirit continue to uplift countless lives, including mine. Your dedication, humility, and faith-filled leadership are a powerful reminder of what it means to serve with purpose and passion.

Thank you, Nav Chhinzer, superintendent at Peel Police, for your dedicated service, leadership, and commitment to creating safer, stronger communities. You are not only a role model and source of inspiration but also a brother and cherished family friend—your support means the world to me and my family.

A special acknowledgment to Donny Sandher, Director Manager at National Chalo Freshco: Your leadership, dedication, and quiet strength have been an inspiration to me.

Thank you, Nina Dhillon, for your trusted expertise and support as an accountant. Your attention to detail, reliability, and sound financial guidance have been invaluable. I truly appreciate your professionalism and the peace of mind you bring through your work.

Local Business Champions & Community Builders

To Mustafa Al-Siaudi, owner of Palm Bites, thank you for your generosity, creativity, and commitment to quality. Your premium date-based treats and luxurious gift boxes not only taste incredible but also reflect the care and excellence you bring to every detail.

To Parminder Gill and Jas Gill: Thank you for your trust, support, and friendship in business. Your kindness, professionalism, and genuine care are truly appreciated.

To Rawal Singh: It was a pleasure meeting you—wishing you continued success.

To Lisa and LeRoy MacDonald, owners of Le Delice Bakery on Lorne Park, thank you for spreading joy through your heavenly baked goods and welcoming space. Your passion for your craft is evident in every sweet bite and every warm smile.

You

Yes—YOU.

I know what you're thinking: Did she forget me?

Not.

If your name is not mentioned here, please know that your presence, support, and influence have not gone unnoticed. You are an essential part of my story, whether through a kind word, a helping hand, a smile, a prayer, or simply walking beside me on this journey.

If you were part of my life, even for a moment, I appreciate you and carry your impact in my heart and throughout my journey.

From the bottom of my heart, thank you.

About the Author

Pam Pabla is the award-winning author of *Unshakable Leadership,* and a respected leader with over 25 years of experience in the insurance industry. As the Owner and CEO of Pam Pabla Insurance and Financial Services Inc., a Desjardins Insurance Agency based in Mississauga, Ontario, she is known for delivering personalized, client-focused insurance solutions with excellence, integrity, and care.

Pam leads a dedicated and knowledgeable team who shares her commitment to protecting what matters most and serving clients with compassion and professionalism.

A Chartered Insurance Professional (CIP), Pam previously taught Chartered Insurance Professional (CIP) courses with the Insurance Institute of Canada, and proudly served as an ambassador for the Career Connections Team at the Insurance Institute.

Earlier in her career, she worked in real estate and co-founded Myo-Serenity Yoga, reflecting her entrepreneurial spirit and passion for holistic well-being. She has also contributed to her community as a youth soccer coach and mentor, consistently leading with humility and service.

At the heart of Pam's mission is a passion for empowering others to rise as *unshakable leaders*—those who lead with accountability, responsibility, and faithfulness. She believes true leadership begins with character, vision, and the willingness to serve.

She champions a life of balance—personally, professionally, and spiritually—to build lasting influence and legacy.

Pam resides in Canada with her family, where she continues to lead her agency, support her team, and inspire individuals through her faith-driven message of leadership, transformation, and purpose.